GAMEKEEPER

GAMEKEEPER

John Foyster and
Keith Proud

DAVID & CHARLES
Newton Abbot   London   North Pomfret (Vt)

British Library Cataloguing in Publication Data

Foyster, John
  Gamekeeper
  1. Gamekeepers——England——History——
  20th century
  I. Title II. Proud, Keith
  639.9'5'0924   SK505

ISBN 0-7153-8841-X

Typeset by ABM Typographics Limited, Hull
and printed in Great Britain
by Redwood Burn Limited, Trowbridge, Wilts
for David & Charles Publishers plc
Brunel House   Newton Abbot   Devon

Published in the United States of America
by David & Charles Inc
North Pomfret   Vermont 05053   USA

Contents

TO LISA

Foreword

I first knew of John Foyster when he was serving with the 7th Hussars at Barnard Castle, and when he left the Army he came to Raby as an under-keeper for a while. He left us to widen his experience, but I was very pleased that he accepted my offer to return here as head keeper in 1977.

Being head gamekeeper here, and no doubt elsewhere, requires far more than the name suggests, and the basis for success is a wide knowledge of country life and an understanding of people. Perhaps it is a paradox, but the quite often lonely life is combined with one of public relations. Tact, good judgement, and a pleasant manner are therefore as important as the more obvious technical skills. But indeed as technical knowledge increases in game conservation, the gamekeeper must be aware of this, and he cannot rely alone on an instinct for the job, and on inherited skills. The Raby Estates' conservation policies demand a fine balance between various needs, and a part of the responsibility for this falls upon the head keeper and his department.

John Foyster has done well to achieve this balance, and he has now widened his interests and is able to present to the public a picture of what is going on in the countryside through his regular broadcasts on BBC, and now, through his book, a description of the gamekeeping techniques which he had learnt in his early working life.

The Lord Barnard
Raby Castle

7

John Foyster today,
outside Raby Castle

Introduction

An old man who could control even the biggest farm horse by using the bleached bones of a dead frog, a mole-catcher who used the same penknife to cut an apple and to measure out strychnine, and a lovable villain who loved to torment bees; these were just some of the fascinating characters encountered by the young John Foyster in the first five years of his working life as a gamekeeper's lad in Suffolk. He was just fourteen when he started work in 1935.

Fifty years later, John is now head keeper to Lord Barnard on the vast Raby Estate with its magnificent medieval castle in whose hall the Rising of the North was planned.

For twenty-three of those years, John Foyster was a regular soldier with the 7th Queen's Own Hussars and he has pursued the gamekeeper's craft in Surrey, the West Midlands and, now, Durham as well as in his native East Anglia. The skills and knowledge he uses daily were learned in those formative years when he was known as Boy Johnny, the keeper's lad.

1
Schooldays

It was not quite light as I approached the snare, but, even so, it was obvious that what I had hoped to find in it was not, in fact, there. The snare was empty but it had been sprung, posing a considerable mystery.

The puzzle, or rather the events leading to it, had actually begun several days earlier at the start of my daily round at Benacre Broad when three dead cygnets were found floating on the water. They were no more than a week old and I had seen them the previous day swimming contentedly with their mother. The villain who had engineered their sudden demise had to be an otter and the sight of those dead birds so incensed me that I vowed he would kill no more, for this was senseless killing where the victims had not even been eaten. There was a well-worn otter-run from a nearby dyke to Benacre Broad and the otter in question probably travelled this route. There was a chance that he could be snared, so I fetched some strong brass wire and returned to set up a trap. Using as a bender the branch of a tall willow tree which overhung the run, the device was set. I drove a strong peg into the ground and then constructed a trip mechanism; pulling down the strong branch, I secured it to the peg and made a loop of wire over the run. Any animal which put its head into this loop would trip the trigger and be jerked up into the air, its neck snapping instantly.

11

It was early the following morning when I returned to the snare site to be confronted by the lingering mystery. The expected otter was absent but the snare had obviously been sprung because the wire loop was several feet in the air. On closer inspection, I saw something on the ground below the loop. It was white and curved — a meerschaum pipe with a face carved on the bowl. A couple of yards to the right lay a black Homburg hat. It had obviously been there all night for it was covered with dew, and all around the reeds and grass were disturbed and flattened, showing that something or somebody, caught in my snare, had struggled to escape from it; a pedestrian, crossing an area which was very much out of bounds to all but the Benacre keepers, had surely put his foot into the otter snare. I say 'his' because very few ladies of my acquaintance wore Homburg hats and smoked pipes, but, conversely, I knew only a few men who did so. Which of these few would have been abroad on Benacre in the dead of night? Who would have needed to travel that route? Even during the day few did so; whoever the nocturnal traveller was, he must have known the path well for it was difficult to negotiate at the best of times with some of its route passable only by stooping.

At the keeper's hut, I looked more closely at my two finds. The hat was not uncommon, but neither was it commonplace. Inside it were two pieces of information; it was a size 7 and, proclaimed on the band inside, was the name of the maker, Martin of Cambridge.

The meerschaum pipe carried no such identification. The face carved on the bowl was that of Lord Kitchener, and the bowl and lower stem were well yellowed, showing that the owner had smoked the pipe over a period of time. Could this owner, then, have been a military gentleman? There was one further clue, for the pipe had a new mouthpiece, the old one possibly having been damaged or chewed through.

The matter of returning hat and pipe to their rightful owner placed me in a quandary. It was highly unlikely that they belonged to a poacher for none of my acquaintance had ever sported a Homburg. Discretion is a virtue which should be the

Wrentham reading room and village shop c1900

watchword of every good gamekeeper; he sees, hears or is told much which is best kept to himself, and, although he is the eyes, ears and nose of his beat, he should only rarely be the mouthpiece.

A few days later, I went to the shop in Wrentham where I always bought my cigarettes and asked the proprietor whether he sold meerschaum pipes. There was little call for such a luxury as that in our area, he said, but confided that he always did have two in stock, 'just in case'. He looked surprised when I asked to see them but as the shop was not busy he went off into the back, returning a minute or so later with two small red boxes. Each contained a beautiful pure white meerschaum, one perfectly plain and the other bowl carved with a face, but not that of Kitchener. I asked whether he had ever stocked such a pipe as I had found. He had indeed, he told me, but there was no demand for them in 1936. He reminded me that the war had ended nearly twenty years before and he had not carried a Kitchener pipe for more than ten years. Then a smile came to his face. The last such pipe to leave his shop, he recalled, had been bought by the present vicar, but that was years before, in

13

Benacre Park from the Lowestoft Road

fact so long ago that he could not remember precisely when. Further conversation revealed that the vicar still bought his tobacco at the shop, 3oz a week, and that he must have bought two or three new pipes since the Kitchener meerschaum. He had also bought some new mouthpieces and a tobacco pouch. I left the shop with the distinct impression that if I had stayed much longer I would have known more about the vicar than his wife did.

The vicar had certainly not been in Benacre Park at dead of night and the two other men who wore Homburgs were equally innocent. One was confined to a wheelchair and went out only when there was somebody to push the vehicle, and the other gentleman was a solicitor who travelled to Wrentham a couple of times a week. Neither of these men smoked a pipe, so they were neatly eliminated. I needed to know where the vicar bought his hats and that fact was soon established. At bell-ringing practice a few days later, the vicar was also in church. He had laid his coat and hat on the back pew and, since there was nobody to see, I looked inside and read 'Martin of Cambridge', size 7. The mystery hat belonged, or had belonged, to the vicar; of that there could now be little doubt. Furthermore, his hat was obviously almost brand new, so somebody else must have acquired one of his old hats.

A few hours later in the Horse and Groom, I joined a group of friends who were listening to a tale that was the source of a great deal of amusement. I gathered that the cause of the laughter had been one of the men telling how he had seen old Prod, a local character familiar to us all, getting off a bus in Lowestoft dressed in a ridiculous way. He wore his usual old boots, trousers tied with string at the knees, an overcoat which had seen much better days and, on his head, a black Homburg hat. The narrator had walked beside Prod for a hundred yards or so, trying to draw him into conversation, but to no avail. Prod was a very peculiar, very independent old man, and not given to idle chatter. If he had nothing to say, he said nothing, being of the opinion that it is better to keep your mouth shut and let people think that you are a fool, rather than open your mouth and prove it.

16

He had explained this philosophy many years earlier to me, and I still find it sound advice today.

Another member of the group in the pub had seen Prod later that same day. He was sitting in a café in Lowestoft having a cup of tea when he spotted the old man going into a tobacconist's where he had stayed for at least ten minutes. When he emerged he had looked very pleased with himself and was examining something held carefully in his hands. He had then hobbled off down the street and out of sight.

Arriving home late that evening, I retold the tale to my father, and he knew where Prod had acquired the Homburg. It had been on a stall at the church jumble sale two weeks earlier but, having unaccountably not been sold, it was put with the rest of the unsold jumble outside the hall. Father had seen Prod pick it up, try it on and walk off with it. You could always tell when Prod was about for he smoked a stubby black clay pipe which he said he filled with Magpie Shag tobacco, but which we suspected to have been dried herbs from the hedgerows. It really was a dreadful aroma. Whenever he smoked in public there was always a clear space around him, but he rarely appeared in public anyway. The vicar had gone up to him at the jumble sale and whispered a few words in his ear. Prod put the old pipe into his pocket and went off into the back with the clergyman. When they reappeared, Prod was beaming. I have always wondered if the vicar gave him the meerschaum to stop him smoking the awful old clay pipe.

Prod was an inveterate old poacher and it was almost certainly he who had tripped my otter snare on one of his illegal forays onto Benacre land. I shall never know the truth but if it was he then the story has an ironical twist, for I had learned to set such snares when I was just a lad, and the man who had taught me was old Prod. Had he been, therefore, hoist with his own petard?

The year of my birth, 1921, was not particularly conspicuous as far as the history books are concerned. King George V had been on the British throne for eleven years and the Prime Minister

17

Thatched cottages, Mill Lane, Wrentham

was the Welshman, David Lloyd George. The Great War to end all wars had been over for three years. I was the ninth of the Foyster children. We lived with our parents in a thatched cottage in the small East Anglian parish of Covehithe in East Suffolk. The parish was, and still is, on the Benacre estate and is about 3 miles from the larger hamlet of Wrentham.

My early days as a schoolboy were very happy times. We had a little village school in Wrentham and I walked to it and home again every weekday no matter what the weather. Even on my first day at school I went alone although I was only five years old. My parents must have reasoned that, since I knew the way and no harm would come to me on the journey, there was no need for me to be accompanied. My earliest teachers were ladies, who left no great impression on me, but, when I was ten, I went into the headmaster's class. He was a splendid man who had been a regimental sergeant major in the Suffolk Regiment during the Great War, and when we left school we all carried away with us something of his remarkable character. Mr Spall was very strict but very fair. In appearance he was tall and robust with short brown hair, like a scalped shaving-brush.

Our favourite lesson was gardening, but the allotments were about 2 miles from the school. To travel there we would form up in four ranks, our spades and hoes at the slope, and then we marched off up the road singing patriotic songs. Our rendering of 'It's a long way to Tipperary' sounded wonderful to us. Our arms were swinging and our heads were up as Mr Spall led both us and the singing. He was obviously proud of us although he would never have admitted it. Looking back, we marched as well as any body of men I ever encountered in the army.

Mr Spall was a hard man who showed no favouritism, tolerated no fooling, and would have been more hurt than angry if anyone had let him down, although we never did so knowingly. We were frightened of him but we respected him, and he was a great one for fair play. Our education consisted of learning to read and write and some elementary arithmetic. A lad in the country in those days knew that his future lay as a farm-worker or with employment in some local craft, and he did not need to

Boypower in the school garden

be educated to university standard for that. I was to wish on several occasions later in my life that we had been better educated, but our education seemed adequate at the time. I could not, in any case, understand why I needed to be able to calculate the area of the headmaster's lawn when I could see perfectly well how big it was.

Mr Spall was a wonderful story-teller and used to tell us tales of the Great War; in fact, in our history lessons we usually manipulated the conversation in such a way as to persuade him to recall some of the events of that great conflict.

My father, earlier in his life, had been a gamekeeper but had moved to the Benacre estate to take charge of a team of Suffolk punches, these big horses and their management having always been his first love. At Benacre, his immediate employer, a tenant farmer, was Sidney Wright.

I had two brothers, one of whom, Ernest, died early, having had the top of his head blown off in the war. A silver plate had been inserted in his head, but the shock of his injury caused him to contract diabetes and he died when I was only seven years old. It was my first experience of death. My other brother, Clifford, worked as a rabbit warrener on the estate. One of my brothers and a sister had died before I was born, and my remaining sisters, all older than I, were Hilda, Peggy and Dorothy.

When not at school, I used to spend nearly all of my days away from the house, either walking or watching the wildlife. We lived quite near the sea, and my favourite haunt was the beach. I could walk all day along the coastline from Lowestoft to Southwold. Between the beach and the firm land were the marshes, and in that watery zone there must have been a different bird to each clump of reeds. To be in the marsh area at daybreak was something to behold; everything would come to life, building to an extravagant scream of noise. I would arrive on the marsh well before dawn with a pack of cheese sandwiches stuffed in my pocket.

The great thing to look for along the beach at that time was amber. I found a piece once, about the size of an egg, and took it to a jeweller in Lowestoft. He gave me 30s for it although I later discovered that it was really worth £5. I was happy with what he had paid, however, for it seemed a fortune to me.

It was amazing just what you could find on the beach. I once found a dead body which had obviously been in the sea for a long time. The eyes had gone and the nostrils had been eaten away, too. On learning later that this was the work of shrimps, I have never like them since. I walked all the way to Southwold to report my gruesome discovery to the local coastguard. I showed him where the body lay, but before he would hand over the statutory 5s reward, I had to touch the corpse as the finder and claimant. Although I was only twelve, this was no real hardship when there were 5s at stake, so I laid my hand on the unfortunate sailor.

On the marshes there were 'marsh-men' whose job was to look after the dykes, or 'deeks' as they were known locally. These were fairly wide but sluggish streams which became regularly clogged with reeds which the marsh-men had to remove. Prod was one of these men, a 'rum owd boy' but a tremendous character, who lived all by himself on the marshes. His name was George, but he was always known as Prod, and I visited him whenever I could. He took his nickname from the fact that on the marshes in the summer time there are thousands of bees' nests and he would go round prodding with a stick until he found one. Then he would go off to a piece of high ground and collect an armful of dry grass which he carried back to the nest. He set fire to this grass to try to smoke out the bees. It was a funny sight but a regular one — old Prod running like mad across the marsh with thousands of angry bees behind him, his hat in hand wildly flapping them away. He was always doing it, although I never did work out what perverse pleasure it gave him. He was rarely stung despite deserving to be.

Prod was an old rascal who lived all alone in a wooden hut. He was obviously a poacher, but the keepers knew that he was harmless. He showed me how to make my first catapult and it was a precision job. The crotch was carefully selected from privet and the piece he wanted had to be the perfect shape. The pouch was of very soft leather and the elastic was about ¼in wide. Prod taught me how to use this weapon and then sent me off to practise until I became perfect at it. He also made me a sling. He was a marksman with his, but I could never get on with it.

Prod was very superstitious. The tales he would tell made my hair stand on end. There were certain areas around the marshes he would never go near. He claimed that there was a presence in these places. There was one particular farm, the track to which had a pond beside it. Prod loved to tell me how he was walking there one night when, suddenly, he realised that he was not alone; there was somebody, or something, walking beside him. Sure enough, when he turned to look, there was an old fellow with a big black hat and long frock coat. The figure walked beside him for several hundred yards and then it just was not there. On other occasions, Prod claimed, you could stand on the track near the pond and hear this old fellow snap his tobacco

23

box, presumably a ghostly version of one of those round silver boxes with a hinged lid on a spring. He was perfectly serious when relating these tales. At about the same time, my brother Clifford came home late one night in a very agitated state. This was completely unlike him. We shared a bed and to my surprise he ran upstairs and jumped into bed fully clothed and with his wet boots on. I asked what the matter was and after some coaxing he replied, 'Don't ask me. I can hear the chains rattling still.' He would never afterwards talk about this incident, but he had been working near Keene's Farm. One day this farm burned down and it was said that, after the fire, the ghost was never heard nor seen again. The description of the ghost by those who had encountered it fitted perfectly the description of farmer Keene, the tenant of the farm long before my time but within living memory. At the time of the fire, the tenant farmer there was a man by the name of Hoseason. He then moved to Oulton Broad where he became Broad-master in charge of the waterway and its boats. The name of Hoseason is still well known on the Broads today.

My mother was extremely religious, a kind woman, but very narrow-minded, as were many in those days. She was, nevertheless, an absolute dear. She set great store by her Sundays and was a keen member of the Mothers' Union, but she was a firm believer in these apparitions. She tried to make me go to Sunday School and although initially I went reluctantly, I soon wriggled out of it. I certainly went to the Sunday School teas which was, perhaps, not entirely fair since I was not a regular attender, but they did put on a very good tea which satisfied my constant hunger. I was invited to the teas through the good offices of my Uncle Harry who was a church warden and whom I made it my business to see whenever a Sunday School treat was in the offing.

My mother used to play occasionally on my weakness for food. She was a marvellous cook who could produce a big meal from almost nothing. I was probably the greediest one at home, although I was growing the most. If she made sausage rolls, I always picked the biggest one. Another great favourite of ours

Benacre Hall today

was a little beef pudding which was made in calico cloth. These puddings were like small dumplings to look at, and they were delicious. Naturally, I would always snatch the biggest, and sometimes there would be an extra big one which I would scoop onto my plate. Inside there would be a turnip but no beef at all. Mother played a similar trick with the biggest sausage roll, inserting, instead of sausage meat, two clothes-pegs with just a little meat showing at the ends. Whenever I fell for these tricks of hers, everyone used to roar with laughter, including me.

Mother's baking day was Friday and she used a Dutch oven. It was made of brick and was 6 or 7ft long, and about 3ft wide, part of it in the kitchen itself and the rest extending beyond the outer wall. It was heated by faggots which could be bought from the estate and the oven we had held a complete faggot. Once the oven was lit it had to be used to capacity and mother made all sorts of things like bread, sausage rolls, salt shortcakes and rusks. When the oven's iron door was open there was a red glow inside and the bread and cakes were pushed in with long tools, especially bought or made for the job. There was a rake to excite the embers and a spade to feed in the bread. There was a definite skill in knowing precisely when the food was cooked, for the oven had no thermostat. The food was then removed with the long spade and tipped carefully on to the wooden kitchen table. Coming home from school on Fridays, I could smell the baking half a mile away and the smell of freshly-baked bread certainly made me hasten my step. My treat was to be given a crust from the new bread, covered in butter which melted into it. Mother baked enough to last us a week, but if we ever ran out there was a bakery in Wrentham where we could buy 'baker's bread'. The rusks, which were something like scones but savoury instead of sweet, were delicious with a piece of cheese.

Just as we were always amused when my mother's practical jokes worked on me, so Prod and I had many a laugh, too. He had never been to school in his life and he told me that he could read print but not 'real writing'. I doubt now even his ability to read print and he certainly could not write. He used to smoke Magpie Shag in his old black pipe, and to make the tobacco go further he would add to it dried leaves from the hedgerow. The resulting aroma, especially in a confined space, was something akin to a dying garden bonfire. Prod's hut was a most aromatic place. He always had at least half a dozen red herrings hanging up which had probably been there for weeks. These were his iron rations in case times became hard. On rare occasions he would somehow acquire a small joint of beef which he would dutifully put in the oven to cook. He had a habit of forgetting about his cooking and must have become used to eating his own 'burnt offerings'.

In the early summer the farm people went down to the marsh with the horse and reaper to cut rushes which they used for litter. This was a job which took all day so, having started early, they stopped for their 'nineses', as they called them, then their lunch, and then their 'fourses'; old Prod was always present for this annual ritual and he was a great one for dozing off at 4 o'clock. He had only to sit down and he was asleep, lying there with the palms of his hands upwards and snoring merrily. Somebody had heard that if you pour a little cold water onto the palm of a person's hand when he is asleep it has a remarkable effect on the bladder. The lads decided to try it out on Prod, and, although he could only read the print and not the writing, by goodness he could swear. The air was blue for about ten minutes for the pouring of water had had the desired effect.

Old Prod was in his sixties when I knew him. He actually died when I was away from home several years later. I shall always be grateful to the old man, not just for making my catapult, but for showing me how to make snares and to use them properly, particularly to catch rabbits. I used to take my catapult to the beach where there was an enormous ready-made supply of perfectly round pebbles which served as catapult ammunition. I practised with the weapon until I became quite deadly and could easily hit a moving rabbit.

My catapult once almost landed me in trouble, and all because I was such a good shot. An old fellow called Jocky Allum lived in the village, an old seafarer who used to indulge in occasional bouts of heavy drinking. He would go on the bottle for two weeks at a time and he would take a short-cut across the fields to travel from his house to the Five Bells at Cove. We came across him one day as Donald Durrant and I were travelling home that way from school. The footpath ran along the top of an old sand-pit which was also bordered by a high hedge. Jocky must have felt the call of nature for, as we passed the sand-pit, we saw him there with his trousers around his ankles. Donald asked if I had my catapult with me. He had no need to say any more and I could not resist the temptation. Taking a quick aim from behind the hedge, the howls of rage announced that I had hit the target. We took off like bullets and, although Jocky could not possibly have known who his assailants were, we avoided him for weeks afterwards in case we were discovered.

Jocky's brother was another old sea-dog and he was always known as Tow because he had a head like the cleaning rod of a gun. He used to wear very large ear-rings and looked just like a pirate. Many people in the area had pierced ears and wore ear-rings, claiming that this helped their eyesight. He had the broadest Suffolk accent I ever heard. His son was also known as Tow and he sat next to me at school. Although he was like his father in most ways he was, nevertheless, a remarkable scholar. Old Tow loved to work on the herring drifters out of Lowestoft and when he had money at the end of a trip he, too, liked to spend it in the Five Bells. Outside his cottage hung his old leather sea-boots, oiled ready for the next voyage.

Prod insisted that before I set up a snare I should know exactly where to put it; to this end we studied a rabbit's run. He told me that where the animal's feet touched the ground there would be slight indentations. From this we could work out where to set the snare so that when the rabbit tore along its run and tripped the snare, the wire would go around its muzzle and not its neck; thus, when it was trapped so suddenly, it would turn over and break its neck. Although country lore like this has stayed with me down the years, it is, nonetheless, more difficult to snare rabbits today than it was then, because in those days rabbits had a destination. There were more root fields then, turnips, sugar-beet, and the like. The rabbits would leave the wood or wherever they had their burrows and rush to their feeding grounds, usually in one of these fields, and the faster a rabbit runs, the more easily it is snared. Today, they seem to come out of a wood and hop around, never leaving the vicinity. In my youth, if 200 snares were set, you could be certain of taking 150 rabbits. In those days there were rabbits by the thousand for this was long before the introduction of myxomatosis.

It was in this context that I first came across the local beat-keeper, Friday Thrower. One day he searched me and took the catapult out of my pocket. In those days keepers were very powerful people on the estate and I was sure that I was not going to get my catapult back. He looked at it, studied it and then, remarking how well made it was, he returned it to me, saying,

'Well, Boy Johnny,' for everyone called me that, 'I don't think you're going to do me much harm with that.'

I had met Friday Thrower before, but on that day I went away with the impression that he liked me, and it was soon afterwards that I went to work with him and learned from him more than anyone else ever taught me about keepering.

I did not apply for the job as keeper's boy, but it was assumed that I would work on the estate along with the sons of the other workers. The agent came to see me one day and told me about my future now that I was almost ready to leave school. The agent was not a man I liked, a pompous fellow full of his own importance, but he did set me on the right road in life.

As I left school, the headmaster said that if ever I wanted to talk to him he would always be available. We bumped into each other many times over the next few years as he was out for a walk and I was on my rounds and we always had a good talk, frequently reminiscing about things like the school football team for which I used to play. The school had its own bicycles on which we rode to away matches; it was nothing in those days to ride 16 miles, play a hard game of soccer, and then ride home again. Schoolboy soccer then was not as skilful as it is today and we played much more aggressively. Our team was never more than average but I enjoyed playing centre-half. The school provided us with blue shorts, but we played in our everyday shirts and always used our own boots which we looked after very well. The game as we played it was more or less an absolute determination to get the ball into the opposite goal and we did not always stick rigidly to the rules. It was always a hard game but we loved it.

Another of our pastimes was sea-fishing from the beach. We could never afford to buy a proper rod so we used to make our own tackle; we used to buy our lines, of course, and the hooks. For the lead anchors, because in sea-fishing you need a heavy anchor with claws to prevent the line being washed ashore, we dug for bullets. During World War I there had been an army firing range quite near the sea and we used to dig the lead bullets out of the butt at the end of the range. We then melted down the lead and ran it into a wooden mould, putting stiff wires through it so that when it set we had the perfect anchor weight. We had to be able to cast our hand-lines over the first breaker. Sometimes we ran four or five lines, pegging them well down on the beach. Not having a proper rod, we never really knew when we had a fish on the line, so every so often we pulled in one of the lines and there was usually a catch there, a whiting or a flounder, a dab and, occasionally, a cod if we were lucky. We caught many dogfish but we always threw them back as they were not good to eat. The great thing was to catch as many fish as possible, especially dabs, take them home and have a lovely tea, fresh from the sea. We would stand in the freezing cold all day for that meal, for we always fished in the winter months, never in the summer. For bait we always bought lugworms; these cultivated worms were always far better than those you could dig up on the beach. On Sunday mornings there would be up to forty or fifty people on the beach, some with expensive rods, but we had just as much fun, and success, as they did.

There was other fishing to be had, in the rivers, but in that East Anglian low ground they were full of predominantly coarse fish which I did not like to eat as much as sea fish.

Looking back now, it is amazing how all the strands which made up my childhood came together in those early teens to shape the young, but growing, John Foyster, Boy Johnny. My childhood came to an abrupt end the day I began to work as the keeper's lad at Benacre.

2
A Beginning
in Spring

During the thirties, children could leave school a little before their fourteenth birthday if they had a job to go to. I left in the spring of 1935, my certificate of elementary education proving that my time had been spent relatively fruitfully. There was nothing special to mark my leaving school. The headmaster was told about my job and as the examinations were over, he had no objection to my leaving early.

I reported for work to Friday Thrower, the keeper, and the first job he gave me was to act as a mobile bird-scarer. The spring-sowing had been drilled and my job was to keep the pheasants away from those fields, as they would come out of the adjacent woodlands in their hundreds and attack the corn. Their favourite times for these forays were early in the morning and late in the evening. At first it seemed an easy job but I soon realised that it was very hard. It was easy enough to move them out of one field but, as soon as you moved to the next one, back they would come to continue their meal. If the job was not done properly there would have been great bare patches where there should have been corn. Without a mobile scarecrow like me the estate would have lost large acreages of corn to the pheasants. Even though shooting had finished in January there were still hundreds of the birds. People seeing such a sight today would assume that there had been no shooting the previous winter.

A gamekeeper — late nineteenth century

I had no special clothes for this work, just a strong pair of boots, a waterproof coat which kept the weather out, and a cap. With the aid of a stick and various devices, like clappers and my catapult, the pheasants were driven away. The old cocks especially were cheeky devils and they certainly led me a dance. It was a very long and tiring day which extended from daybreak to late afternoon. Suffolk is prone to north-east winds during springtime and when I sat down for a rest a hedge was always a welcome protection from their bite which could be bitterly cold and often carried snow showers. I used to watch the herons in a wood known as the Long Covert. They were very active about then. I occasionally saw one of the rabbit warreners or Friday Thrower. In a good spring the corn would quickly push through by which time it was safe from the ravages of the pheasants.

I was too far away from home to return for meals so each morning I pushed some sandwiches into my pocket and took a bottle filled with my mother's home-made lemonade. This was varied with a bottle of cold tea which was also very refreshing. Bread and cheese is a satisfying snack and I still retained my fondness for a good crust. Some estate workers preferred meat sandwiches for their snack. In the scullery of nearly every cottage there was a ceiling hook from which was hung a half pig. The meat could be cut from it as required and sandwiches would be made with enormous pieces of pork between two slices of bread. About 50 per cent of the sandwich was fat which was plastered with mustard.

My constant companion in those days was my little dog, Toto, a sheepdog-whippet cross, whom I had had since he was a puppy. He would come with me into the harvest field during my schooldays when the corn would be absolutely alive with hundreds of rabbits. On one memorable occasion he brought me more rabbits than I could kill which reduced me to tears because I could not keep up with him. No sooner had he dropped one at my feet than he was back with another. All the rabbits caught in the harvest field were laid out and counted. The farmworkers were allowed to take as many as they wanted and the remainder were given to the other people in the field. All the estate workers were given a brace of rabbits every week by one of the keepers as there were more than enough to go round and it stopped people poaching them. In some cottages this weekly meat dole was very gratefully received.

Toto went everywhere with me. At the time of year when all the keepers took their little dogs with them to go after rabbits, they used to arrive at work on their bicycles, dogs' heads peeping from their game-bags. The reason for the dogs being cross-bred was that a pure whippet would have been too timid to enter dense cover in search of rabbits. Our dogs, however, having the long hair of the sheepdog and not a little of its courage, were not daunted by the prospect of corn or even nettles and they had the whippet's speed when the rabbit broke cover.

My salary at this time was the princely sum of 5s a week, an amount which was almost equal to the value of the cigar-butt discarded by the squire.

After the green corn had shown above ground, my next task presented itself. This was to thoroughly clean an enormous pile of hen-coops, the like of which I had never seen in my life.

Common pheasant, cock and hen

When they were carried out of the barn they formed a heap about the size of a house. Friday Thrower was a very particular man, especially where hygiene was concerned, because the best way to combat disease was, and still is, prevention. He insisted that every coop had to be scraped and cleaned and then lime-washed. There was little in the way of disinfectant at that time so they were thoroughly scrubbed with soap and water and then lime-washed. The long wooden nest-box compartments also had to be cleaned. Although it was a soul-destroying task, I derived great satisfaction from doing the job well. On some days the weather was fine but on others there was a biting wind and the job could be very hard on the hands. Sometimes the ice on the water had to be broken before I could start work.

As soon as the coops were ready we prepared the nesting yard. There were two long lines of nesting-boxes facing inwards. Ted Martin, the underkeeper, helped me with this job. He was a grand man who had a wide range of experience. During World War I he had worked on trawlers and had stayed with the fishing fleet for a time after hostilities had ceased. I learned a lot from him, including how to use traps. Friday Thrower was also a great trapper, as all the keepers were then. He once told me that a good keeper could do his job without ever picking up a gun. He explained that a trap, set properly, did its job while we were asleep; it never tired as we did but was always there and ready.

Ted Martin took me around with him and taught me how to tunnel-trap, although at that time it was known as through-hole trapping. Gins were then perfectly legal and were deadly for catching all types of vermin. On our round, or beat, several hundred of these gin traps were set, snaring an enormous number of pests. Each trap was steel-jawed, had a base plate and a strong spring. There is no doubt that they were very cruel. The jaws, with fierce teeth, would be about 4in square and the spring about 9in long. You had to press the spring down, put the trigger across and lift the plate. The gins were also used in rabbit holes. Setting these traps was an art and many a nip and nasty bruise could be suffered from being a little

The tunnel or through-hole trap

careless. Unlike the traps used today, these had no safety catches. We had two very thin sticks, known as prickers, each about 12in long. When soil or sand was thrown in the hole on top of the plate, these prickers were used to prevent the trap from going off; the plate was held with a stick underneath it and then, when the plate was completely covered, with the other stick on top the trap was set 'tittly' so that the least pressure on the plate would set the trap off. In the hole where it was being set the trap needed room to spring up and, in the case of a rabbit, it would catch the animal well up on its legs but did not kill it outright. This was the feature which made the gin so cruel. Nobody, however, wanted to be unduly cruel so the first job of the day was to check the traps. They were set along the sides of small streams, where there were gateways and in woods, and there would be one in every hedge leading from the woods, especially on what we termed the partridge manor.

I loved being near the hedgerows with their delightful smells and especially that given off by sweetbrier. Most of the hedges in East Anglia were full of this.

In the corner of many fields baited-traps constructed of brushwood would be laid against a tree. A way in would be formed and half a dead rabbit exposed on a spigot near the tree; the gin would be set in front and completely in the open. The idea of this was to catch poaching cats, either domestic cats which had turned wild or ordinary household cats which travelled from their homes to the wood. So many troublesome cats were caught in this way that I was afraid of cycling through the village for fear of retribution from housewives who had lost their feline pets.

The bicycle, which made getting around so much easier, was supplied by the estate. It was big and heavy like a postman's bicycle but with no basket on the front. I would often cycle off with two or three dozen gins on my back.

Gins could be used to catch foxes, too, but these predators were rarely a problem in East Anglia. They did not stand a chance even though there was no hunting in the area. If a fox had been reported as far as 12 miles away not a keeper around would rest until it was caught. From 1935 until the outbreak of war I only heard of two foxes in the vicinity and they did not live long. Game and pheasants were so dense that a fox would have created havoc.

April heralded the start of one of our busiest times, rearing the pheasants. Friday despatched me on my bicycle with a good supply of sacks to search for broody hens. I went around all the farms with a bag of money in my pocket, and paid 2s for each bird. There were thousands to choose from, but they had to be selected carefully. The best time to visit the farms was in the evening when the other hens had gone off the nest and they were not laying. The old broodies were, however, still on the nest.

I used to come back with as many as I could carry. Ted Martin, meanwhile, had cycled off on the same errand but in a different direction. After several such journeys we would have about two hundred broody hens. Into each nest-box we put several china eggs and each new bird was placed into her own nest-box with her own china eggs. Eventually, we had long lines of nest-boxes full of broody hens in a situation where they were ready to receive the pheasant eggs.

Logically enough, the next job was to collect those eggs. Friday, Ted and I searched the woods, for in those days there were no laying pens in East Anglia. Only the head keeper kept penned pheasants; in an aviary he had pure-bred Chinese and Old English black-necks and, sometimes, Mongolians. From these he collected the eggs and mixed them with the other eggs we had collected. This was to improve the blood lines and prevent over-inbreeding in the wild strain.

We walked the woodland in a line and it was soon obvious that Friday and Ted could see far more than I, even though my young eyes must have been keener than theirs. I had not yet obtained my 'woodcraft' and I would not be able to find the eggs until I 'got the colour'. Pheasants' nests were scattered about the woods but the knack of spotting them had to be learned. It was not long before I picked it up.

This method of collecting eggs was peculiar to East Anglia. With the large number of hen birds left on the estate after the shoot the woods were absolutely full of nests brimming with eggs and it would have been folly to have left them. Several hens used to lay in one nest and these eggs could not be wasted. Teams of us, as many as four, would quarter the woodlands and pick up enormous quantities of eggs. In other parts of Britain the method of propagating pheasants was for the keepers to make 'pheasant-catchers' to collect hen pheasants which were then placed in laying-pens. Here they were fed daily and with them were cock birds at a ratio of five females to one male. When the eggs were laid they were collected daily and stored ready to go under broody hens. The East Anglian method was, however, only possible where vermin were kept down to the lowest possible level, and on Benacre and the neighbouring estates a nest was rarely molested.

We walked back from the woods, our pockets bulging with eggs and our baskets full, too. In a day we collected hundreds which we took back to a big thatched shed where there were trays filled with damp sand. Friday stood the eggs in this and turned them conscientiously every day until he had the number he required. The reason for turning them was that if the egg lay flat the embryo would settle down and eventually go to the bottom end and stick to the membrane next to the shell. Turning the egg each day prevented this. There is no need to do this when the hen sits on her eggs because she continually turns them.

By the end of April or the first days of May we liked to have the first big batch of eggs under hens so that they hatched by 1 June, the incubation time being twenty-four days.

There were two long rows of nest-boxes and opposite each box would be a tethering peg. These were in a perfectly straight line and beside every three pegs there was an earthenware water dish so that when a hen was taken off her nest she was carried to the peg to which she was tethered by a piece of cord around her leg. This allowed her to walk around relatively freely, to eat the handful of maize thrown down for her and to have a drink of water.

The procedure was well ordered. Friday would take the hen off the nest and hand it to me. I would then pass it to Ted Martin who would tether it, and this was repeated all along the line. The great thing to remember was not to take too many hens off at any one time because it was a time-consuming job and the pheasants' eggs, once placed under the hen, had not to cool too much, especially in the early stages of incubation, or the embryo would die. The hens could only leave the eggs for ten minutes at the most for the first two or three days. It was also important for each hen to empty herself before she was put back on the nest, otherwise she would have become restless. At that stage the job would take nearly all day.

Searching the woods for the eggs using my egging stick was a great pleasure. This was a piece of hazel with a crotch on the end and with it I could reach into cover and part it to find nests even in the dense clumps of nettles. Some birds nested in the open and others did so under bramble thickets. Pheasants' eggs range

39

in colour from brown to green to blue and olive drab and they are always well camouflaged. There were so many pheasants at that time that frequently more than one hen was laying in each nest. I once found a nest containing forty eggs, but a single pheasant hen lays about fourteen eggs before she goes broody and settles down on them.

We had to be careful and decide whether the bird was still laying or had gone broody. Normally, a broody pheasant will protest violently if you try to remove her eggs once she has settled to hatch them. Broody pheasants were, therefore, left to hatch their own eggs. Unfortunately, pheasants are the worst mothers in the world and have been known to hatch their chicks and then, in really foul weather, trail them through the wet grass so that they catch a chill and die one after another. A hen pheasant who brings up six of her fourteen chicks in the wild is doing very well indeed and we were quite happy if she managed four. We do sometimes see large broods of wild pheasant chicks but they usually vary between three and five. Not all chick losses were due to parental stupidity; some were down to predation from the likes of weasels, stoats and hawks.

Chicks reared under the supervision of the keepers fared much better. Under a large broody hen like a Light Sussex we would place twenty eggs while a Rhode Island Red could manage fifteen. An added bonus from all these broody hens was that when their pheasant chicks were about five weeks old they needed no more care from her and she started to lay eggs of her own. We had hundreds of these eggs which were sold, but eggs were cheap then.

We had between three and four hundred hens on our pheasants' eggs. Our procedure for looking after the daily needs of the broody hens continued until the eggs were at the point of hatch. A few weeks prior to this we went to one of the farms to collect a horse and cart, a rearing field for the pheasant chicks having already been selected. Although we called it 'the' rearing field, it was actually two large fields. The best rearing fields were not those with lush green grass but with the scrubby sort which did not grow too high. We dropped the coops in straight lines across the field, each coop 20yd from the next, and then we had to set them. The first tool we needed to do this was a rammer, part of a tree trunk with a handle attached, and with this we rammed the ground tight. The main purpose of this was to hammer down mole-runs because these were often used by weasels which travelled along them and came up inside the coop to steal the young chicks. Another reason for ramming was to make the ground as flat as possible.

After the coops were all set out, the woodman would turn up at the field with waggon-loads of tree boughs. Several boughs were placed behind each coop to protect the chicks from hawks.

The rearing field was frequently quite a distance from the nesting yard where, by now, the young pheasant chicks had hatched. To transfer them from one place to the other we put the broody hens in sacks, while the chicks had a more comfortable journey in a basket lined with flannelette over a hot water bottle. A hen was placed into each coop and she was given fifteen chicks to mother. It did not matter which chicks we gave her since she did not, at that stage, know the difference. Gradually, we filled up the three hundred coops.

Also on the field were two keepers' huts and a cookhouse where all the food for the birds was cooked. An added complication was that the food could not be put into a trough and left there because after the sun had been on it for twenty minutes it would go sour and if the chicks ate it they would sicken and die. We had to be expert enough to give the chickens just the correct amount which they would eat completely.

During the rearing period Friday Thrower lived in the field and did not leave it. In his hut he had proper mixing bowls made out of zinc and he did all of his own mixing. For the first week the chicks' diet consisted of hard-boiled egg, yolk only, pushed through a sieve and mixed with fine No 1 biscuit meal. Its brand name was Gilpa and, depending on the weather, the mix was of a wetter or drier consistency. Wet weather was not healthy for young chicks because they would drink a lot of water which would scour them. As the chicks became older, their food was made coarser so that from being a week old a little rice was

41

added to the food. Cooking the rice required a special technique which was demonstrated to me. The cooker was a brick affair with iron bars across the top and a galvanised tin roof. It was fuelled by wood delivered by the woodman and sawn by me, as the youngest worker, into the correct lengths. The fire was always laid the night before so that Friday could light it when he got up, which was always well before daylight. He had enough egg and biscuit meal from the previous evening for the first feed which was given at 6 o'clock in the morning to keep to the pattern of feeding the chicks at 6 and 10 o'clock in the morning and 2 and 6 in the afternoon. The broody hens, however, were fed only once a day.

At the same time as the rice was introduced, some No 2 biscuit meal, not as fine as No 1, was also included. The most important aspect of boiling the rice was knowing just how much water to add to it. After coming to the boil, it was left to simmer when all the remaining water would be absorbed. It was properly cooked when it felt soft but there was still some of the hard core in the middle. It was perfect when a little cold water could be splashed on it and each grain of rice would separate. What had to be avoided was a big mass of sticky and congealed rice. As the chicks grew, increasing amounts of rice had to be cooked. In the third and fourth weeks, dehydrated grains of meat, called greaves, were added to the diet. In the evenings we shot rabbits which were skinned, boiled and minced and a certain amount of that meat was added to the chicks' food. It did not take much time to collect a dozen rabbits each.

By the end of the third week, egg yolk had been completely eliminated from the diet and replaced by plenty of meat and coarser biscuit meal with the addition of corn, also boiled, and barley meal, all worked by hand into the food. The chicks were only fed three times daily by the end of week five.

During these important weeks even a lad as lowly as I had to spend some nights on the rearing field. Friday Thrower was an excellent pheasant-rearer and a stickler for hygiene. All the pots and pans had to be scalded and cleaned daily and no food was ever allowed to go sour.

Towards the end of the rearing period barley meal was mixed into the food to give it more body.

One of the most trying aspects of pheasant-rearing was the morning and evening ritual of liberating the chicks from the coops and locking them safely away at the end of the day. In the morning we went to each coop, took down the shutter and flung it well back so that it would be lying there in the evening when it was time to shut them up. Sometimes friends would come along to help with the evening ritual as it could be a tiresome business. We would walk in a straight line with nobody getting ahead of anyone else. Towards the end of the fifth week the young pheasants become very touchy and a person who was clumsy with a shutter was a distinct liability because the slightest noise would disturb the occupants of the next coop and even beyond and cause them to come out to investigate such an unwarranted disturbance. If this happened it was a long time before they would go back inside. They were not allowed to stay out all night and anyone who caused such an exit was not very popular with his colleagues. I was not the only one to make this mistake on occasion, and we all took a turn at being in the doghouse. We would creep up to each coop — three hundred in all — as quietly as we could and secure it for the night. Once the birds had been thus secured, and only then, would we retire to our own beds. We often heard the eerie trill of nightjars at sunset and saw them swooping low over the coops in their silent, mothlike flight.

Had the birds not been safely enclosed each night, many would have fallen prey to their natural enemies. Owls and other birds would fly onto the coop and rattle the roof with their claws. If the door was not secure the young poults would come out and be snatched by the enemy, for enemy he was. The keeper was ever vigilant for these marauders and one of our tricks was to dig in a post about 100yd from our hut and lash a rifle onto the side of the hut. On top of the post was placed a tin onto which the rifle was aligned. The tin was then removed and the rifle securely clamped and loaded. At odd times through the night one of the keepers got out of bed and pulled the trigger. The next morning there was often a dead owl lying beside the post. All owls were fair game in those days and we boys would add to our pocket money by cutting off owls' feet and taking them to the jeweller who gave us 5s, a week's pay, for our trouble. He then used them to make brooches. Occasionally, we caught an adder and sold it to the chemist for 2s 6d for its venom. A firm called Horace Friend would buy such things as mole and stoat skins and pheasants' tail feathers. We first skinned the animals and tacked the skins onto a board to cure. A better price was had if we rubbed a mixture of alum and saltpetre into the pelts to keep them soft. When we had a good number of skins we sent them to Horace Friend and in due coarse a payment cheque arrived. No working people had bank accounts then so we cashed our cheques at the grocer's.

Even though my first year as a keeper's boy passed remarkably quickly, we were all very aware of the passage of time on the rearing field. There was no going off to the cinema or to the pub during those critical weeks for there were always jobs to be done from daylight to dark.

Friday, living in his hut on the field, would be up at four in the morning and it would be eleven at night before he went to

Friday's lodge with large look-out windows

bed. We who were living at home would arrive on the field at six in the morning to find that Friday had all the food in buckets waiting for us. He was a stickler for time and would not tolerate our being late, so we made sure we were there by five to six. I still used the bicycle and brought my breakfast and lunch to work with me, sometimes sandwiches and, occasionally, a couple of eggs and some bacon which I could fry on the fire. At the end of the rearing period I was dog-tired but knew that we had achieved something worthwhile. Those six weeks were not uneventful.

One morning the postman came to the field and told us that he had seen a fox as he was riding past a wood called the Holly Grove. This was almost unheard of in that part of Suffolk. Our first reaction was to check the coverts where we knew there were still sitting birds. What we found terrified us all: hen pheasants had been snatched off the nests and torn to pieces. The same damage was apparent everywhere we went. Together we drove the wood but there was no sign of the fox. Then we heard that one of the farm labourers had seen the animal at another wood and the head keeper, who had now heard about the intruder, arrived with about a dozen helpers including some of the tenant farmers. The assembled gathering of hunters went to the wood and together we drove it. Eventually, almost a week later, the fox was spotted and duly shot. We discovered later that the animal had escaped from a fox farm near Norwich; it was more silvery in colour than the normal wild fox and had travelled about 20 miles from the farm. Needless to say, we could have done without the extra anxiety and work he brought to us.

Kestrels were another permanent nuisance for they would work on a brood of pheasants at one coop on the rearing field and keep at them until there were none left. Not all kestrels were like this, but easy pickings on the field obviously attracted certain individuals. The only protection afforded the young birds was the collection of boughs we had placed behind the coop. Occasionally, a sparrow-hawk would sweep across the field and take one or two birds, but he usually made his appearance when the chicks were nearly five weeks old. He was not too interested in the small chicks, but the kestrel, which could hover above the coops, would take them whenever he could. We were also troubled by little hobby-hawks, small but very swift. They were magnificent birds which also swooped on their prey but did not hover like the kestrel. None of these hawks was protected then and we had to shoot them when they became too troublesome. It is strange, looking back now, to consider that, even though they were shot by all gamekeepers, there were far more hawks then than there are today when they are a protected species. For years keepers have been blamed for the greatly diminished numbers of these birds and yet there are very few about today despite the fact that they cannot be killed. Farm chemicals are, I fear, their worst enemy.

The other big worry on the rearing field was disease. The most stringent standards of hygiene had to be observed. Every bucket, bowl and cooking pot was scalded regularly in a big copper in which boiling water was always available. We always scrubbed our hands well before handling pheasant food.

If disease set in seriously, we did not have the scientific and medical aids we have today. There were no pathology laboratories to tell us how a bird had died. Keepering in those days was far more an art than it is today; now it is largely a science. Some keepers could produce birds far more successfully than others. One man could rear his birds with a success rate of up to 80 per cent while his neighbour could be as low as 50. Most of the success was due to common sense and the rest was down to hygiene.

One disease whose appearance on the rearing field heralded real trouble was gapes. This is a red worm which collects in the bird's windpipe and lungs; a sure sign that the bird is infected is when it starts to sneeze or 'gape', opening its beak wide. They also flick their heads as they try to discard the unwelcome guests. There was no cure for it then. The birds pick up the worm as an egg during wet conditions when there are lots of slugs and worms about. These were, and are, the hosts for the parasites. The chick eats the slug or worm and, unwittingly, the parasite egg. This egg is then incubated inside the bird and

46

when it hatches it makes its way quickly to the bird's windpipe. If the chicks acquired gapes before they were three weeks old, the keeper could lose a large number of birds but, as they approached the poult stage, they were much better able to cope with the worms. They contracted the parasite far more readily once they were released into the woodland where the worms already lay in the soil. Our great desire was to keep the disease off the rearing field where it caused the highest mortality rate.

Our remedies to combat gapes were crude. A white powder was available which we placed in a tin on some bellows; then, after the chicks were shut in the coop at night, the spout of the bellows was placed into one of the ventilation holes and the powder puffed in. The chicks had no choice but to inhale it and although it was not entirely successful it did seem to help them. If the infestation was very serious, a long feather was dipped in turpentine and pushed down the bird's throat. When the feather was extracted many worms would be stuck to it. In very serious cases the worms would actually bore through the windpipe allowing air in between the outer and inner membrane so that the afflicted pheasant blew up like a balloon. It could be helped by picking up the bird, pricking it with a pin and squeezing out the air. Although sheep have a similar worm, it cannot affect humans. Gapes is still rife today but it is no problem since it can be easily cured with modern drugs.

Coccidiosis also existed then but it was called entram. This disease attacks the blind gut of the bird and can be deadly. Most modern poultry food contains additives to combat coccidiosis but in my young day there was no such thing. Hundreds of birds could and did die in an outbreak, but I saw it only once and then not too seriously.

We never saw feather-pecking since it is a disease engendered by intensive rearing, as is what we call vent-pecking. An infection causes the bird's back end to become inflamed. The other birds notice this and peck at it because it is an abnormality. Once the vent is attacked an intestinal stoppage usually follows and the constipated bird dies. What we did occasionally see was a broody hen who had turned cannibal for no apparent reason

47

and started killing the pheasant chicks in her care. There were very few ways to cure this but one man had a callous but distinctive way of doing so. As soon as a hen killed a chick, he took out his knife and, in a flash, cut off one of the hen's toes; his theory was that the hen was so worried about the loss of a toe that she left the rest of the brood alone. This sounds cruel but it most definitely worked and avoided the necessity of finding a new foster-mother for a brood of chicks.

Prevention was the only answer to these rearing field worries since cures were almost unknown.

The greatest problem on the field came when the first batch of poults was five weeks old and the second four weeks, for there were always two separate batches reared, one a week after the other. It was then very difficult to shut the birds in their coops in the evening, but, by keeping calm, we managed it.

At five weeks old, it was time for the first batch of poults to leave the rearing field. The keeper would choose the day after consultation with the farm manager and on the evening of the move two or three farmhands would arrive with the horse and trolley, this being a low waggon without sides. The birds were moved in the middle of the night when they were in the coops. We worked in pairs and had a number of stiff corn bags. One man took one side of the bag, his colleague the other, and they would slightly lift the coop as they slipped the bag right under it, coop, hen and poults. The bag, and what was on it, was then lifted onto the trolley. Some keepers tacked the four corners of the sack to the coop before they moved it, but this was unnecessary. We continued moving our charges until we had a load and then off we went to the woods to release them. Prior to this the rides had been trimmed, a necessity since they had a growth of thick bracken by then, so that the horse and trolley could move along the rides. Every 20yd or so we stopped and removed one coop from the trolley, carefully slipping the sack from beneath it once all was safely on the ground. The coop and its occupants were then safely placed in their new environment. We moved the coops all through the night and refreshed ourselves with beer. Two of the woods we filled on our beat were the Orze

Gates and the Little Orze Gates. The Holly Grove was the new home for a few birds.

The last year that keepers reared their own birds on the Benacre estate was 1935. Thereafter they reared the birds together on one enormous field and then we all lost five or six nights' sleep at release time as the poults had to be delivered, over the course of those nights, to all the different beats.

In the early summer of 1935, on the morning after 'the great transportation', we went to each coop and took the door away. Despite all the disturbance of the night those poults walked out of the coop for their food as if nothing had happened. They were eating their usual moist food which we put out for them but the old hen still needed to be watered. Just as we had moved the coop each day on the rearing field to prevent it from standing on stale ground, so we moved it in the woods. The birds were now fed at six in the morning, at noon and at six in the evening. We still had to shoot rabbits as meat continued to be an important part of the birds' diet. No longer did we have to shut up the coops every night, and although we were safe in our part of Suffolk from foxes, it was still an anxious time. Very soon after being released in the woodlands the poults would fly up in the evening onto the lower branches of the trees. Flying to these roosts gave them nocturnal safety from predators. We could also tell at about that time how many were cocks and how many hens, for the necks of the cocks become dark, but we never worried about the ratio of cocks to hens as the right balance would eventually be achieved by shooting cocks only late in the season. Some of our charges were, however, still in danger. They were the old broody hens who usually stayed in the coop which was no longer shuttered. The hen could still get her head through the bars to take food and water and keepers occasionally found a few headless birds when they arrived in the morning, the culprit sometimes being a marauding dog. The coops were moved onto fresh ground daily. The hens were left in the coops because they acted as an alarm when danger, such as a hawk, was present, and they still had a homing effect on the young poults. During the summer these broody hens were gradually removed until all

Grey partridge and family

had gone and the coops were returned to storage for next year. The poults would by then be firmly settled in their piece of woodland.

The keeper still had to look after his beat as well as coping with the rearing of the pheasants. Partridge nests had to be found for he had to know how many nests had hatched off. He had first to find the nests, which was difficult for me as a beginner as I had not acquired 'the craft'. This was a time-consuming job but it had to be done and the positions of all partridge nests were recorded field by field in the keeper's notebook. An experienced keeper would know, by and large, exactly where to find his partridge nests. The birds were thick on the ground then, in fact there was a pair of partridges to every 5-10 acres. In some fields there were two or three pairs. They are rather peculiar little birds and very clever. They usually make their nest on the side of the hedge opposite to the prevailing wind and in a sunny spot.

Up to the time when a partridge starts to sit on its eggs, which is when there are about fourteen or fifteen eggs in the nest, it covers them when it leaves the nest. The partridge then becomes broody and when it leaves the nest it exposes the eggs, probably to cool and ventilate them; in cold weather, the cock bird will sit on the eggs as soon as the hen leaves the nest. In this way, while the hen is away from the nest having her recreation and food, the cock continues the incubating process. As the chicks hatch, and some come earlier than others because the last eggs to be laid tend to hatch first being the most fresh, the cock takes away the newly hatched chicks from the nest and broods them. The hen stays behind to incubate the remaining eggs. The cock is also very courageous. If that pair of partridges and their brood is threatened by an intruder, such as a dog, the cock bird will leave the family and present himself to the predator; he pretends to be lame and runs around in circles with a wing down, trying to draw the threatened attack onto himself, gradually working away from his family. This ploy is usually successful and the cock is able to fly off to safety.

I once came across a brood of partridges trying to cross a busy road. Cars were roaring along it and not one driver bothered to slow down. The cock bird was trying desperately to get his family safely across and eventually a car ran him over. Partridges are superb parents.

These birds are the grey English partridge but the French partridge with its red legs can also be seen. It is not as common as the grey partridge but neither is it such a good parent. Of all the game birds in the British Isles, the grey partridge is the one to be most admired. There are so many obstacles and dangers before them that it is marvellous how they survive.

As the young partridges come into the poult stage they form into coveys and the keeper then has an idea of how many birds there will be when partridge shooting begins in September.

It was during my time on the pheasant-rearing field that I was properly introduced to the shotgun. The reason for this was, principally, so that I could contend with the predators which attacked the field. I had previously had one or two shots but now I was to be allowed to use the gun properly. As Friday handed the gun to me he stressed that it was a tool, not to be idolised but to be used as an aid. Over the years, and particularly during the war, those words came back to me. In the army I saw just what a gun can do to human flesh and animal flesh, too, and I still regard it as an absolute sin for anyone to idolise firearms. Some young keepers today use the gun far too much. Friday always insisted that he could do his job without resorting to the use of the gun. I have the greatest respect for guns but will not use one except when it is absolutely necessary. I do not have anything against those who shoot birds for sport but I prefer to see a gun used properly if it is going to be used at all. The man who claims that although he did not get many birds on a particular stand he certainly 'smartened them up', is the sort who will shoot at any rising bird; if it is only 10yd in front he will blow it to pieces; if it is a 100yd behind you can see it flinch as the shot hits it, but it is only wounded and will die slowly and painfully. Such men should never be allowed to shoot at live game but should stick to their clay birds which do not suffer if just a piece

Red-legs; French partridges

is chipped out of them. By and large, however, the sportsmen I have known have been very particular about their shooting and have been genuinely concerned if they thought they hit a bird which was not subsequently retrieved. If the man told us in which direction the wounded bird had flown off we would despatch a man with a dog to find it.

My first gun was a hammer, double-barrelled gun, and it was very clean. The choke barrel was on the left with the open barrel on the right. I was instructed always to pull the right-hand trigger first because pulling the left trigger first could set off both barrels, and they were light triggers for it was an old gun. So off I went after rabbits and soon saw one in the distance. Since it was so far away I used the choke barrel, forgetting what Friday had said about that trigger. I fired, and immediately found myself on my back. Both barrels had gone off together wounding my pride, missing the rabbit and teaching me that what advice Friday gave should be not only heeded but also remembered.

That gun, an Atkin, Grant and Lang, was now my responsibility. When shooting was over, it had to be cleaned because the caps in the cartridges were caustic and corrosive and if the gun was left until the next morning without attention the barrels would have been red rusty and impossible to restore to their original condition. It was stressed that a dirty gun was a dangerous gun. With modern cartridges there are no such dangers and today there is no need even to clean the inside of a gun so often.

I soon became proficient with my gun. Nobody can simply take a shotgun and find his way with it, although the person who becomes a crack shot is born to it, not made. People often learn to shoot nowadays with the help of a clay trap, but we had no such aids. Friday simply took me into an open field and explained how to use the shotgun, how to load it, how to mount it, how to follow through the target and shoot in front of it if it moved laterally. Many beginners make the mistake of stopping the gun while they squeeze the trigger, in which split-second the target has gone past and the shot goes off harmlessly behind it. After a time, all of this comes naturally. I missed my targets

WILLIAMSON'S
SPECIAL
Smokeless Cartridges

7/6
PER
100.
Cash with Order.

1,000 Carriage Paid. **Less Quantities** at Special Rates.

Scarlet (English-made) Metal Lined Cases.
Full **Charge Schultze, Amberite, or selected** Nitro Powder.
Guaranteed equal for Strength **and** Penetration to Cartridges
at much higher prices.

C. W. WILLIAMSON,

Advertisement for cartridges, early 1900s

hundreds of times before becoming proficient. I had been good with a catapult and the shotgun is aimed and fired on a similar principle. Practice consisted of throwing an old tin into a fast-moving beck and shooting at that, remembering to aim in front of it. We were never short of cartridges for these were always supplied so that we could shoot vermin and rabbits. Cartridges should never be carried in the pocket but I did so until I acquired a leather cartridge bag, especially made for the purpose.

It is detestable to see deer hit with a rifle bullet but not killed outright and allowed instead to get away. This always happens through poor shooting, for example being too far away to be certain of killing the animal. The bullet should always go through the rib-cage so that, even if it is not an instant kill, the deer cannot possibly escape and the keeper can walk up and despatch it quickly.

Cruelty of any sort is intolerable and no animal should be allowed to suffer unduly. Quite recently, we were stalking deer and a keeper had shot one. I was nearby but not close enough to see what had happened but I then heard the wounded deer screaming. Arriving on the scene I saw that the animal was far from dead, having been shot in the wrong place, and the keeper was attempting to stick the animal. Enraged, I asked curtly what he was doing. He thought that his action was correct but I insisted that no animal should be stuck with a knife while still alive. I almost dismissed him on the spot but gave him a stern warning instead. The correct procedure was to race to the deer and shoot it through the head. Every deer has to be bled immediately but not while still alive. There is a feeling that those who indulge in blood-sports have a cruel streak in them, but I do not believe this to be the case.

The principles I hold today are a direct result of the training I received more than fifty years ago from Friday Thrower as we approached my first summer as a keeper.

3
Gentlemen
be Damned

In Old English the word *pocca* meant 'a bag', and the medieval French verb *pocher* meant to 'place in a bag' or 'to steal game and fish'. These, then, are the multilingual origins of our word 'poacher', a romantic figure for over two centuries in the eyes of many but, in reality, a villain of the first order and a cruel, thoughtless breed. They have been called 'gentlemen of the moonlight', but gentlemen they most certainly are not. There is, today, a large lobby against blood-sports, but no such outcry against the poacher is ever heard. It would be expected that a gamekeeper would adopt this stance, the poacher being, it is always imagined, his sworn enemy. It is true that the two do not see eye to eye. In my years as a keeper I have seen too much of their gruesome work to have any respect for them, but I have learned a great deal about their ways and shall always be grateful to Ted Martin for he it was, in quieter moments on that rearing field in 1935, who gave me my grounding in the poacher's ploys.

We were able to have these chats only in wet weather because then we did not have the time-consuming task of filling and afterwards emptying the water bowls of the broody hens. Ted instructed me well and explained the tell-tale signs for which to look. Game coverts were full of pheasants and the poachers would have a trained dog, usually a cur, and this they would set off to 'tree' the birds. The dog achieved this by rushing about wildly, causing the pheasants to fly up into the trees. In doing so, the pheasants made such a noise that the keeper could not ignore it. Once the poacher had treed the birds he used a catapult or air gun to bring them down.

Another method was to steep grain or raisins in strong spirit. The poacher would find the keeper's feeding places in the woods and then scatter the grain which he had previously steeped in spirit, usually whisky or port, or even methylated spirit. A few hours later, he returned to the wood and picked up with ease the stupefied, drunken pheasants.

The keeper could detect the presence of poachers by looking for pheasants which were choking. Poachers would soak peas in water and then pierce them with a needle. They would then take some stout horsehair which they threaded through a pea, snipping it off close to the pea, leaving just a fraction exposed. These peas were then scattered over the feeding area where they were picked up by the pheasant, the horsehair causing them to stick in the bird's throat. This meant that it could not swallow properly so it would desperately try to rid itself of the pea or peas, becoming progressively weaker in its struggles so that, eventually, it was so debilitated that the poacher could simply pick it up.

Another crafty but cruel dodge which was used particularly at breeding time when the cock pheasants were especially pugnacious involved the poacher's use of a specially trained bantam-cock. It was armed with steel spurs and sent into a wood where there were numerous cock pheasants. As this was their territory they would immediately attack the intruder who would defend himself and half kill the pheasants with his long spurs, leaving the wounded birds as easy pickings for the poacher, badly mauled but still saleable.

There was also the use of the gun at night. One poacher would act as decoy and go to the far corner of the keeper's beat and fire a gun well away from his accomplices. The keeper's natural inclination was to hurry to the noise of the gun, and while he was away the other poachers would shoot as many pheasants as they could bag. One poacher made his escape by dressing up as an old lady pushing a pram. When approached and asked if 'she' had seen anything, she replied that she had and then sent the keeper in the wrong direction.

The noisy poacher was another example. He would enter the cover and shoot two or three pheasants which he would quickly hide, along with his gun. He would then walk off up the road whistling. Nobody would expect a poacher to be so noisy and, if he were stopped, he would admit that he had heard some shooting but could not place quite where. When everyone had gone away, the poacher would return to his birds and gun and go on his way, amply rewarded for his noisy subterfuge.

Normally a gun is too noisy for poachers but not too noisy for a gang of them. On a windy night pheasants roost lower than usual in the trees and always facing the wind as they do not like it to blow into their feathers. A crafty poacher would approach on a windy night from behind the birds, preferably on a fairly well-illuminated night. He would tie a handkerchief on the end of his gun to form a crotch, a pair of 'rabbit's ears'. In the semi-darkness he would aim his gun until the dark shape of the pheasant nestled well between the rabbit's ears; nine times out of ten he would shoot it out of the tree. This would not even disturb other pheasants nearby since they hate to be disturbed at night and nothing will make them leave their tree on a windy night. They will fly well on a moonlight night but they do not like a dark one. The ideal poacher's night is when it is dark and raining very hard, and they prefer the winter months.

On a stormy night with high winds and heavy rain, the experienced poacher would go to work. In those pre-war years there were no high-powered air rifles but there were air guns with a pump. These guns could fire a lead ball but they were not as good as shotguns since they fired a single ball, not spread shot, and required greater accuracy.

Ted Martin also taught me how to study footprints as these often give away useful information about the poacher. The size of the man and his state of health can be estimated from the prints he leaves. If the length of his stride remains regular it means he is walking steadily, but if the distance between them shortens then he is moving more quickly, possibly after he has been disturbed. If the footprints show that his toes turn out-wards he probably has some foot trouble and is not as active as he would like to be. The man to beware of is he who has a good, lengthy stride with his toes pointing straight ahead; he is obvi-ously fit and active. The poacher with pigeon toes is unlikely to be very nimble. A keeper should always be extremely wary of very large and deeply indented footprints as they probably be-long to a big, strong man.

If a keeper had this knowledge about footprints, then so did the poacher and he learned to walk on short stilts. The keeper could still detect the holes these left but they were more difficult to spot and it was almost impossible to learn from them any-thing about the build of the poacher.

Ted Martin also described another poacher's trick which was probably an old wives' tale but he swore it happened. This was 'smoking the pheasant' in a tree. For this the poacher needed a long bamboo pole which could be broken down into sections as he would not want to attract anyone's attention, particularly the keeper's, by carrying such a strange object. To the end of his re-constituted pole the poacher would attach a tin, such as a cocoa tin, into which he had placed some sulphur. The sulphur was lit and the smoking tin pushed up to the wind side of the bird. The sulphur fumes were then blown onto the pheasant, choking the bird and causing it to fall out of the tree. I have never known this method to be used but I would have thought that, since the roosting bird hides its head in its dorsal feathers, its nostrils would be unaffected by the smoke. Still, Ted was a wily old bird himself, and swore that it was one of the poacher's tricks.

Perhaps the most deadly poaching method was the use of the single-strand rabbit wire. Normal Bungay snares consist of five strands of brass wire but the poacher separated these to take just one strand which he formed into a single snare. He would then observe how pheasants were using a field and where they were going through a hedge; he would then place his snares at their passage points. The bird would bend its head to go through the fence, and there was a good chance that it would put its head straight through the snare loop. It would then pull and struggle and eventually choke itself. Since there was just one strand of wire, such a snare would be virtually undetectable by the keeper, and they are used even today. Prosecution for the use of these snares was then, and is even now, very difficult. One of our keepers found a whole set of such snares along a fence in one of which was a pheasant struggling to escape. He determined to wait until the man who had set the trap returned to collect his prey. About an hour later a man appeared who knelt down to retrieve the pheasant and the keeper approached and accused him of poaching. The 'poacher' was brought before the magistrate where he explained how he had seen the unfortunate pheasant struggling in the snare and had knelt down to extricate it. Imagine his surprise, he explained to the bench, when he was accosted by the keeper and accused of the felony. He was acquitted while the unfortunate keeper was given a severe reprimand for allowing the pheasant to suffer unnecessarily.

Cage traps were also used by poachers, most notoriously the lobster pot. This is a small wire-netting cage with a lobster-pot entrance. The pheasant, which is probably the most unintelligent bird, could walk in but was too stupid to escape. The older cock pheasant, however, is an exception and can be very cunning.

The poacher was always the keeper's enemy; he was no fool, had never to be underestimated and would frequently go to extreme lengths to fill his bag.

Poaching was not an immediate problem once we had liberated the young pheasants from the rearing field into the woodland. In July and August 1935 our lives settled, more or less, into a routine of feeding those birds and keeping them in the woods. They were fed three times a day and the food still had to be cooked and mixed. It was a much coarser food now, much of it being kibbled, coarsely ground maize which was either cooked or soaked. A proportion of rabbit meat was still included in the diet; this was also cooked but the amount was gradually lessened since the pheasants in the wood were able to eat insects and grubs and so acquire their own protein needs.

60

The other constituent of their food at this time was barley meal. The business of working this meal into the cooked grain was quite an art; if it was a wet day and we gave a damp feed they would tend to 'squitter', in other words, pass loose motions, and in this state they were more vulnerable to disease, so on a wet day they had to be given a drier feed. In between preparing the feeds and giving it to the birds there were other jobs to be done.

One morning, after checking the traps, I was returning to the cottage where our keepers' hut was situated. The blackbirds were getting very excited. They are a great friend to the keeper as they announce the presence of a predator and their shrill chirping announced that there was an intruder nearby. It was obvious that the predator was of the four-footed kind because the blackbird has two warning calls, one for the four-footed intruder and one for the winged variety. A spaced call of a repeated 'chow' sound signifies that there is unwelcome movement on the ground, while if the bird is very excited, flitting from tree to tree with its notes very close together, then it is a winged enemy. Thrushes and other birds also take up the alarm and, if you watch and listen carefully, you can work out which direction the predator has taken. In this case the threat was some distance away but it was, it seemed, coming towards me. I stood behind a large tree to see the intruder. Eventually, a complete litter of stoats appeared. Considering that our woodland was heavily set with traps it was amazing to see such a procession. I had frequently been advised to avoid a litter of stoats when it is on the move for it was said that they are likely to attack the jugular vein, and it cannot be pleasant to have a big stoat hanging from one's neck. In this case the mother was about 6yd ahead of her brood, altogether seven of them, all of which were larger than she. Her tail was completely vertical and had she spotted any danger she would have waved her tail quickly from side to side and her young would have scattered in a split-second. In this case she had no chance to give any warning. I had her in the sights of my shotgun and killed her. Before a second shot was loosed off the youngers had all scurried into nearby rabbit holes. The burrow had at least six holes to it but I reasoned that, if I waited long enough, at least one or two would reappear. This they did, but before I could raise my gun they had gone back down the holes. I was a novice in this situation and was not sure what to do. It was a mile or more to the cottage and there were no traps handy but, being determined that these vermin should not escape, I removed my hat and stuffed it down one rabbit hole, blocked another with my jacket, yet another with my shirt and stood in just my breeches and vest. There were still more holes to block so I took off my socks, thinking that nothing would get past them. I chuckled at that thought for my feet were distinctly aromatic after having been enclosed for a while in my boots.

On my return, Friday was in the hut preparing the food for the midday meal and he was both perturbed and amused at my strange appearance. He roared with laughter at my explanation and gave me six gin traps with which I returned to the burrow. Six stoats were caught in the traps which left only one of the

Feral cat cage trap

litter free, but although the traps were reset, the last one got away. My victims were hung proudly on the keeper's gibbet as was the custom in those days. It was my first brush with stoats and I was highly satisfied with my work for that litter would undoubtedly have accounted for several broods of pheasants in their time.

Soon afterwards, Friday told me that the local warrener, the rabbit catcher, had complained that a big black feral cat was in the area. These cats are the domesticated variety which have left home, have no intention of returning and live in the wild. They are very cunning. Friday sent me to find and despatch this cat which apparently was living in a field of kale and ruining the rabbits caught in the warrener's traps, moving from one trap to another tearing the rabbits to pieces. This was destroying his livelihood as he sold what he trapped to the butcher, but the rabbits had to be intact.

I went off on my bicycle and silently approached the spot, known as Church Field. I looked over the hedge and to my utter astonishment there was my quarry sitting in the kale. I took my gun and shot the creature, an enormous cat which weighed, as I later discovered, 13lb. There seemed no point in taking it back so I stuffed it down a rabbit hole and returned home. Friday commented on the speed of the operation as he had not expected to see me until late in the afternoon. About a week later Friday came to see me and I could see that something was obviously wrong. Apparently, Dick Plant, the warrener, had complained that the cat was still causing him trouble. They wondered if it had been shot because my return had been so quick on that particular day. Friday insisted on seeing the evidence so we cycled to the place in question. I was not very pleased at having my word doubted. We searched for a long time and it was beginning to seem that we would not find the body. Eventually, however, I found the right hole and pulled out the dead cat. Friday looked at me, somewhat shamefacedly, and admitted that although he had doubted my word on this occasion he would never do so again, and he never did. The matter of the feral cat interfering with the rabbits was never mentioned again.

The warrener was probably hedging his bets for he was not allowed a gun. The system in those days was that the rabbit-catcher would go to a farmer and offer him a price for the rabbits on his land. He paid the agreed amount and then set about catching what he had paid for.

I had started to smoke by then. I used to take some of my father's tobacco and roll it in a piece of tissue paper. One cold day I was sitting beside the kitchen range warming my feet when my mother gave me ten cigarettes. She thought that they would do me less harm than the ones I was rolling myself. We had a wireless by then and the tune coming from it on that occasion was 'Red Sails in the Sunset'.

Often we went around the fields in search of the annoying little owl. It was first brought to this country from Rome by a member of the English aristocracy and I have frequently wished that he had left it there. It is not a pleasant bird and in Suffolk it lives mostly in and around the hedgerows. A dead tree with a conveniently sized and shaped hole is a favourite nesting place. Once one of these owls has started to attack a brood of partridges it will not rest until all are eliminated. These owls are also louse-ridden. We sought out these birds by banging a likely tree with a stick. When the owl or owls came out they would be shot.

After the harvest was gathered at the beginning of August our next job was the bushing of the fields. The woodman would deliver waggon-loads of bushes from the woodlands and these he would scatter all over the stubble. The purpose of this operation was to prevent poaching by netting. At the same time as we bushed the fields we also drove in wooden pegs with turned-over points because although a determined poacher might clear part of the field of the bushes we had scattered he would not find these pegs as easily.

In order to try to net partridges the poachers would watch them at last light for they knew that at that time of day a covey of partridges will suddenly rise up, fly to the centre of the field and then fall to ground there. They do this to ensure that no fresh scent is on the ground near to where they are. They then roost on the ground in a circle, their heads facing outwards. There might be three or four coveys in one field, sometimes even more. Having observed exactly where the birds were, the poachers would approach with a net up to 50ft long and a thick rope along the bottom to weight it. Two men, one at each end, would then walk towards a covey and trap the birds by throwing the net over them. It was a deadly way of catching partridges.

In the second week of September, the official partridge shooting began but it did not concern me as a junior keeper in my first year. I was not allowed to go on the shoot but had to stay behind to tend the pheasants, which were still in the covers. I did not learn, that first year, the fine art of partridge driving, a difficult technique grasped by some but never learned by others. For a short time Ted Martin helped me, but as there became fewer things to do for the pheasants Ted returned to his principal job of catching rabbits. Then I was on my own.

Towards the end of September I was coming away from the woodland and over a piece of ground which was covered in mushrooms. Six youths were picking them and I had no choice but to tell them that they were trespassing and to ask them to leave. They obviously had no intention of doing so and, almost before I realised what was happening, I was surrounded by the six of them. They were all older than I, all had sticks, and soon I was fighting for my life. Fortunately, I had a big ash stick with which to defend myself and eventually they ran off. Had they persevered, they could have overcome and seriously injured me. When I saw that they had dropped their mushrooms, I jumped up and down on them in anger thinking that, even if they did return, they would not enjoy their spoil.

This was not, unfortunately, my only experience of violence; later that same year we had trouble from people with lurcher dogs. My beat was near the foreshore and people would come along the beach with these trained dogs which they sent onto the adjoining land. The lurchers were so well trained that they would pick up hares and take them back to the beach. One particular night when out with all the keepers I was told to wait in a gateway and shoot any lurcher that appeared. Further down the

A shot at partridges, early 1830s

field in another gateway was the local policeman, a ferocious fellow. We used to refer to him as Kronje because he resembled the Boer War general of that name. He was an enormous hulk of a man, at least 17 stones in weight, his hair cut like a Prussian, ½in long all over, and he had deep wrinkles in his neck. His bicycle had a double crossbar to take his weight.

After about two hours, I heard a slight noise behind me. I half turned but then something hit me beside the ear and I fell unconscious. One of the poachers had caught me perfectly with a heavy stick. A policeman had seen the incident as it was a moonlight night and he chased the two men for about 2½ miles. They ran onto the marshes where there were dykes but here he jumped on one of them in the water. Both poachers were prosecuted but I was not called as a witness. My souvenir of the fracas was a lump like an egg on the side of my head, but I was back at work the next morning.

The most fascinating person I met during my first year at work was the man who used to lead the great entire, the big stallion. He was a little man called Cal and he travelled from farm to farm in a small pony and trap with an enormous Suffolk Punch, all done up with braid and brasses, behind it. He stayed for a time at each farm while the stallion served the mares. Cal owned the animal and charged a stud fee for each mare it served. You had only to look over the stable door for the animal to lay back his ears and bare his teeth. I always felt that had I dared to go in he would have eaten me.

One day I asked Cal how it was that, simply by speaking two or three quiet words, he could easily handle this great monster. 'Oh,' he replied, 'there are ways and ways,' and he explained that if you really want to befriend any animal you should take a slice of bread and sweat it under your arm for a while before feeding it to the animal. It was a long time, however, before he revealed his greatest secret. He pulled out a small wash-leather bag from his jacket top pocket and said that it contained his secret. It took me even longer to persuade him to reveal its contents. He told me to watch the next time there was a heavy thunderstorm with torrential rain for it might 'rain frogs'. I was to collect some of these little creatures and carry them to a stream. Next I was to find a holly bush beside the stream and thrash the frogs against it until they were dead, at which point they had to be hung on the tree and left to rot until only the small bones remained. The bones were then to be gathered and thrown into the running stream. Most would float downstream, but a few would actually travel against the flow. These were to be retrieved and cleaned before they were put in a bag and kept on one's person. When Cal opened his bag, there, inside, were some of these small bones. Although I never tried the experiment, the old man assured me that, were I to do so, no animal would ever harm me. It obviously worked for him. It was definitely white magic and even if it was mere superstition, the old country people swore by such charms.

At about this time I met Georgina, a kennel-maid in one of the big houses, the Cedars, where she looked after seven or eight spaniels. I was not very confident with girls having had little contact with them, apart from a few at school. Georgina always smiled nicely at me when I cycled past her, although I was shy and rather awkward. We had been at the same school but she had left first, being slightly older than I. Eventually, we began to talk to each other and went for walks together and from time to time we even 'went out'. When the war began we went our separate ways. She joined the WAAF and after a friendship of just four years I never saw her again.

I had little free time because much of a keeper's work is done in the evenings and very early in the mornings. Some of the keepers were funny old lads. One of them complained that life seemed to become harder and harder in the long days of summer. Every time he sat down, he said, he fell asleep; it was a long time from 4 o'clock in the morning until 10 at night. When asked why he did not take a proper rest from 12.30 until 3 o'clock, he replied, 'Good Lord, I couldn't do that. What would the boss say if he knew I was at home and asleep at that time of day?'

I replied that, surely, his employer would understand the pressure he was under. He would have none of it, however, and was so conscientious that he would work all through the day every day and run himself completely down. Such workers were very good at their job and had no thought of slacking. They would never have thought of asking for overtime although they worked for a pittance.

As the shooting season drew ever nearer the keepers' work became harder, but this was the season of the year which would show whether all the work had been worthwhile.

4
Don't Ask
What's in
the Pie!

Partridge-shooting started during the second week of September. Some of the harvest fields had been cleared though it was not unusual for partridge to be driven over stooks in the field.

Friday Thrower explained that he would take part in the partridge-shooting, which lasted from Monday to Friday. This meant that there would be a house-party at the hall and the guests would shoot the six beats. I was, therefore, to be left in charge of the pheasants in the woods which still had to be fed three times a day and carefully watched.

Looking after the pheasants was a routine job, but what had always to be borne in mind was that the object of rearing them was to have them all available for the shoot. Pheasants are birds of the wayside and field, and woodlands are not their natural habitat. They are great wanderers and love to ramble all over the place, not worrying even if they do not return. There is a craft in keeping the birds where they are supposed to be.

An overfed pheasant is a menace to the keeper for if its crop is full it will wander further than if it is hungry. The crop is a reservoir whence the food trickles through to the gizzard where it is ground up before passing into the stomach. A full crop provides food for twenty-four hours.

The reason a pheasant wanders is that the food it can find in the wild is more attractive than that provided by the keeper.

Pheasants love berries, like blackberries, and they will gorge themselves on acorns, swallowing them whole, until their crops bulge with them. This was the reason we continued with the moist-feeding, with very little grit included in the diet, right up to the day of shooting. Before pheasants can digest hard and dry food they need the correct amount of grit in their gizzard which acts as a mill. The muscles in the gizzard then grind the food into a paste which goes into the stomach and is absorbed into the system. Some people fed whole maize to pheasants, swearing that it was the best food for them. They fed it to them hard and were then surprised at the birds' reluctance to take to the diet, the reason being that they had not enough grit to digest it. Although the moist food we gave the pheasants was easy to digest, this did not alter the fact that the acorns from the oak tree four or five fields away always seemed to taste better to them than those which fell from the oaks in the cover.

Much of my time was spent tending the birds and although they did not stray anything like as much as do the birds today, they still kept me busy. Today, they are reared artificially and put down into pens. When they are let out of the pens, they wander as far away from their home covers as possible. We spent all day and every day dogging them back.

In 1935, if the pheasants strayed too far away, I took my dog and gave them a fright to turn them back. Wherever the birds came from, they always travelled in one or two directions. Knowing where these exits were allowed the keeper to be there to turn the pheasants back. Year after year the birds travelled the same lines as if somehow compelled to go in those directions. The greatest danger of straying occurred in October. Every keeper had his own method of keeping the birds in the areas he wanted them to be, concentrated in certain woodlands because in those days they liked to put up a lot of pheasants over the guns on shooting days. Some keepers were better at holding their birds than others. I watched Friday going to great trouble with feeding the pheasants soaked corn. He would fill a copper with damp corn and build a very low fire under it. Then, from a little bottle, he carefully measured out a few drops which he added to the corn. He then replaced the copper lid, making the vessel airtight, and let the mixture simmer for twenty-four hours. I frequently asked him what his bottle contained, but he would not tell me how he made the food attractive to the pheasants to keep them in his woods.

When he took the corn out of the copper it was decidedly aromatic and had a delightful smell. To it he mixed other foods but the aroma still came through and it had a remarkable effect on the pheasants. Apparently, all the keepers had a 'little bottle' but not all had the same contents. Each keeper claimed that he had the best formula, but the judgement of their potency came on the shooting day.

It was not until after World War II that Friday gave me his formula. He had retired by then and felt that I was mature enough to be given the secret, and since then I have never had any difficulty in keeping and holding my pheasants. I still use it today to great effect. It was no wonder that old Friday had a well-deserved reputation for having heavy concentrations of pheasants on shooting days. What was very important was not to add too great a dose as this could make the birds sick, nor had it to be used too early.

Keepers in those days had no scruples and Friday told me to watch carefully for black oats when walking the hedgerows. Black oats are very difficult to see but pheasants can see them and eat them. Their primary use in the 1930s was as horse feed but they are rarely seen today. Seeing them along a hedgerow suggested immediately that one keeper was trying to tempt away another's pheasants. Even rival keepers on the same estate would try to tempt birds from their colleagues by laying a fine trail of black oats. The week before shooting began the keepers had scarcely any sleep, so busy were they in guarding their beats. The idea was to put up at least a thousand pheasants from a single drive on shooting days because that was the trend in those days.

We had to be careful not to be over-vigilant in keeping the pheasants inside the cover because a bird chased back as soon as it stuck its head out of the cover would never gain any confidence and would be a very bad flyer. We would therefore let the birds stray a certain amount, but just far enough so that they would return for their feeds. The magic mixture used by the keeper on the food played a vital part in this process because pheasants have a very keen sense of smell. Allowing them to stray this little distance makes them good flyers on a shooting day, having more confidence because they have seen the outside world. They have known places to which they can fly and if birds being driven from cover have an objective where they have been previously they will fly high and strong. If they do not know where they are going, then they are very timid flyers and will try to fly back into the woods from which they have just been driven. Two or three fields from the cover is as far as they should be allowed to stray.

At Benacre the first pheasant shoot was early in November and it consisted of a full week's shooting. Gunpowder Plot day was the predecessor of the first day's shooting which was always a Monday.

There were always eight guns for a shoot and each gun had a loader. The ladies sometimes accompanied the guns and on rare occasions a lady would be included as one of the eight guns. Even today there are always eight guns for a shoot and the keeper has to provide stands for those eight. The guns, who were the squire's guests, usually stayed a full week, but if one had to leave early, his place was taken by another gun who joined the party. I was a very lowly member of the Benacre staff in 1935 and did not know who the guests were.

My contribution to those first shooting days was very limited and unimportant. I was a stop and was sent to the corner of a wood at 8 o'clock in the morning. My job, quite simply, was to stop any pheasants from leaving the wood at that point and to wait there until the keepers and beaters went through that piece of woodland. My orders were to dress tidily for the day even though we were not, at that time, issued with keepers' suits. It was not long before I realised the purpose of my station for as the shooting progressed and came nearer flocks of pheasants tried to leave the wood. Had I not been there they would have gone off into the hedgerows and when the guns arrived to shoot that wood, there would have been few pheasants to be seen. I was kept busy all day long chasing the birds back into the wood.

On shooting days we did not have to bring our own lunch which was always provided for the beaters and keepers. The stops, being so important, were not allowed to leave their posts, so their lunch was brought to them. We each received two very large hot beef pies as well as two rounds of bread and cheese and a bottle of the local beer, Adnams Ale, brewed in Southwold. The bottle label showed a fisherman with a sou'wester on his head.

The guns arrived at 9.30 in the morning, the first drive being at 9.45. Hedgerows had already been driven in by the beaters who had also started at 8 o'clock. There were about fifteen beaters actually employed in beating the woods but as many again left as stops. The beaters were paid 5s a day for their work.

The organisation of a shooting day was the responsibility of the head keeper who began preparations three weeks earlier. His prime consideration at all times was to remember that the whole operation was there for sport and it had to be well ordered. The gentlemen present were there to enjoy themselves and it was the head keeper's job to see that they did so. Good organisation enhanced this enjoyment; the gun had to know exactly where he had to go and precisely what he had to do. The head keeper saw to that.

As for the beaters, the captain of the line was always the keeper whose beat was being shot that day. The Covehithe beat, for example, was led by Friday Thrower.

About three weeks before the shooting, the head keeper was invited to the study at the big house where he and his employer would discuss the drives, looking at maps of the estate. The head keeper would mark the position of each gun on every drive, numbering from the right from one to eight. The numbers were decided at the meet. The head keeper would then produce a leather pouch with numbers in it; each gun drew a number for the first drive. If he were number one for the first drive he would move up two places at each subsequent drive,

The loader

becoming, therefore, three, five, seven, two, four and, eventually, eight. The head keeper suggested how the days should be run but always listened to his employer's wishes and accommodated him whenever possible. The employer then gave the keeper a list of the names of the guns who would be present for it was usually the keeper's job to fill in the game register which recorded every day's shooting, what the bag was, who the guns were and how the game was disposed of. The game register was not a legal requirement, just good estate management. At the end of a season's shooting we could consult the game register to see whether the total was up or down on previous years and how much revenue had been earned from the sale of the birds. Some registers were made more attractive by the inclusion of photographs taken on shoot days, which is a nice touch for the benefit of future generations.

Having established how the shoots were to be organised, the head keeper then engaged his beaters. The head keeper at Benacre at that time was Herbert Thrower, Friday's brother, and he was known as Mr Herbert. He was highly respected on the estate and in the area generally. He first consulted the agent to see how many estate employees he could use, people like the woodmen and warreners, with a man or two from the farm. They all had to be told when the shoot days were so that they would be free. The keeper supplemented the estate beaters by employing casual workers from outside the estate and as these men had to be paid, the agent authorised their engagement.

Transport for the guns and to carry the game was also the head keeper's responsibility. The vehicle for the guns was known as the bus; it was pulled by two black horses adorned with braid and ribbons. It was very smart and had about twenty seats. The bus would arrive at the hall, driven by a coachman, collect the guns and take them to the beat for the first drive. The loaders also travelled in the bus as did any of the dogs.

The other vehicle, a two-wheeled cart, carried the game. The tumbrel, as it was called, was pulled by the best Suffolk Punch that could be found and he could haul a load of 2-3 tons. He would wear his polished brasses and was groomed to perfection.

Lunch from the game cart or tumbrel

The cart also carried a brass plate bearing the inscription 'Sir Thomas Gooch, Bart'. The driver of the tumbrel wore his farm smock.

On shoot days Mr Herbert always carried his gun, although he never, to my knowledge, fired it. He also had his shooting stick. Head keepers in those days were known as non-working head keepers. Mr Herbert would supervise and travel from beat to beat but he had an under-keeper to do his work for him.

Mr Herbert and the guns arrived at the first drive and, since there was always a great deal of chattering, he would ask them to keep their voices down or the drive would be spoiled. Eight pegs had been driven in at each drive and the keeper led each man to his position giving him specific instructions. Mr Herbert would say to each gun, 'Would you be good enough to stay here sir, and when the trouble begins would you move onto your stake which is over there?' He then took the next gun to his number, and so on, to the end of the line.

Prior to this the beat-keeper would have used his beaters to drive in the pheasants from the surrounding fields and then he would instruct his men that he wanted no shouting and only to hear one voice — his own. When the head keeper had the guns in position he gave three long blasts on his army infantry whistle. Then the drive began. All of the beaters were experienced and there would be no talking. All that could be heard was the tapping of sticks until each bird rose up and sailed over the trees, soon followed by the report of a gun. Had the beaters made a lot of noise, all the birds would have run forward to escape and they would have been concentrated around the edge of the wood near the guns, a most unsatisfactory state of affairs. The birds must be flushed gradually, one, two or three at a time, by the tapping of stick against tree. As the keepers move forward and more birds take to the wing and sail forward, a well-disciplined band will tap less and the beat-keeper might even stop the men until no birds are in flight. Then it all begins again. The duration of a drive depends on the length of the wood and the number of pheasants there. A drive may last two hours and each drive in those days put up four to five hundred birds. There could be eight drives in a day but it was more usual to have four in the morning and two in the afternoon. The daily bag was between fourteen and fifteen hundred pheasants. What we reared was just a fraction of the number raised by the birds themselves.

When the last bird had been flushed out of the wood and the guns had fallen silent, the beaters would appear at the edge and the keeper would shout, 'All out'. The head keeper would then blow a long blast on his whistle which told the gun to hand over his weapon to the loader because the drive was over.

It was at this point that another important group of people came onto the scene. They were the pickers-up who had been hired at the same time as the beaters. One of them had been put in charge and Mr Herbert had shown him the drives for the day and explained which covers were not to be disturbed as they would be driven later. The pickers-up stood well back behind the guns at different points and watched where the birds fell as they were shot. The ones they were looking for were the runners, those which had not been killed cleanly, and he would put dogs onto them immediately. The dog, having a soft mouth, would pick up a bird and bring it back undamaged; the picker-up would then despatch the bird.

As soon as the drive was over, the game-cart arrived behind the guns and the pickers-up recovered the shot pheasants which they took to the cart. The vehicle was often so full by lunchtime that the driver had to return to the game larder to hang the birds. This prevented them from becoming overheated by being left too long on the tumbrel.

During their movement through the wood it is very important that the beaters stay in as straight a line as possible. Nobody should get ahead of the others because flushing a bird ahead of the line can sometimes result in the bird flying back over the beaters, which is most undesirable. Unruly dogs are not tolerated in the line at all, so if the beat-keeper had brought a dog which was not properly trained he would have been told in no uncertain terms to leave it at home in future. By and large, though, the keepers had decent dogs, and a good dog was very useful indeed where the ground cover was dense.

The dogs used were mainly curly-coat retrievers. These were a cross between a giant poodle and a flat-coat retriever. In its true form the poodle is a very good field dog. Some of the cross-bred retrievers were big animals and the keepers' dogs were not animals to be meddled with. Despite frequent warnings, there was always one beater who would go up to pat the dog, which invariably bit him. They were good game finders, good retrievers, and an excellent night dog, as good as any alsatian we have today. For some reason the curly-coats ceased to be used and were superseded by the labrador. This dog was very fashionable with sportsmen in 1935–6 and keepers gradually went over to them, too. It is a rather sad fact that although there is now a Curly-Coat Retriever Society, as working dogs they are largely useless. Springer spaniels were also coming into fashion during the thirties, but were not yet the keeper's dog they are today.

The pickers-up made sure that no game was left behind, and some of these men were working as many as three dogs to help in the task. The guns themselves were encouraged by the head keeper not to wait at the end of a drive but to leave the collection

Benacre Hall, early nineteenth century

of birds to the pickers-up. Although the guns could help by tel-ling them exactly how many pheasants they thought they had brought down, their estimate was not always reliable. Some could not bear to admit that they had shot nothing on that particular drive and would advise the picker-up that, 'There might be something over there,' even though he knew full well that his bag was nil. However, a good picker-up was used to such ploys and acted accordingly.

The guns, loaders and the rest then moved on to the next stand once the pickers-up had finished, which often meant a fair trek for the beaters who had to walk from one drive to the next. After the morning drives came lunch and on a fine day early in November this was served to the guns out of doors. Trestle tables had been set up in a pleasant part of the wood, table-cloths laid, and the proceedings managed by the butler with a footman to help him serve the meal. Lunch was a full six-course cooked meal, but the main course was usually a rather dubious and sometimes obnoxious game pie. There were some hosts whose lunchtime game pies were notorious, but they were always a

The retrieve; a pointer fetching a shot bird c1830

good talking point. Nor was it a good meal unless it ended with brandy and cigars. All the ladies would turn up for lunch, and if the weather proved to be inclement and unsuitable for an out-door picnic then one of the keeper's cottages or the house of a tenant farmer would be taken over. If the drive took place near the hall the guns would lunch there. Meantime, I was at my place as stop, and, to me, my beef pies were as good as any dubious game pie served on a silver platter.

Lunch for the gentry took about an hour and during the meal the head keeper went to his employer and gave him a slip of paper on which the size of the bag was written. On some shoots it was traditional to have a bet on the size of the bag before lunch and the gentleman who had guessed nearest won the pot.

For the first drive after lunch most of the guns arrived smoking large cigars, and with a rosy face from the wine they had consumed which made them chatter a lot. They were, however, still perfectly sober, for there is nothing worse than a drunken man with a gun. Each gun usually carried a small silver hip-flask, usually containing sloe gin, and this would be passed around.

Gentleman's walking-stick protection gun

At the end of the last drive of the day the beaters would be dismissed. The keepers would then lay out and count the game, including in the total any already taken to the game larder. The birds were always counted in pairs, cock and hen together. The head keeper kept his total to himself while the employer counted the birds. He then went to his head keeper and if their totals agreed all was well but, if not, a second tally had to be done. Bear in mind that they were dealing with hundreds of pairs of birds. Eventually, the correct total would be reached and that number would be entered in the game register and all the birds hung in the game larder. The guns retired in their bus to the hall while the loaders and keepers went to the gun-room taking all the shotguns with them.

The gun-room at Benacre always fascinated me with its relics of the past. Around the walls were spring-guns and man-traps.

Mechanism of the stick gun, early nineteenth century, made by Lang, Haymarket, London

These spring-guns had been vicious weapons operated by trip-wires. They had short barrels and were loaded with explosive caps, nails and various pieces of metal. Any intruder who tripped the wire moved the gun on its swivel so that he inadvertently pointed it at himself and, when the wire was fully taut, the gun shot him. Spring-guns were used mainly in the first half of the nineteenth century, before the time of any of the old keepers. The man-traps had to be set by four men. They were massive gin-type traps and no man caught in one had any chance of escape even if he had an accomplice to help him. I was particularly fond of the old blunderbusses which were hung up.

The shotguns had to be thoroughly cleaned after the shoot ready for the next day. They would be collected the next morning by the loaders.

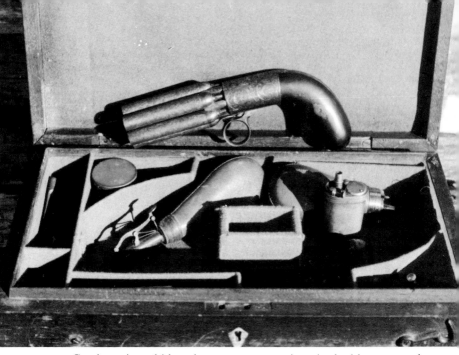

Gentleman's multi-barrel pepperpot protection pistol with accessory box, early nineteenth century

If a large number of birds had been shot one day, a van would arrive from one of the big game dealers so that the estate did not have to concern itself with storing the pheasants. Each guest was entitled to one pair of birds for each day he shot on the estate, although some guests took only one brace in all. The head keeper knew when each guest was leaving and he made sure that the appropriate number of birds was in the boot of that guest's car. There was nothing ostentatious about this facet of the proceedings.

The birds arrived at the game larder where they were unloaded and hung by the neck on a hook. It was very important that the birds were not hung too close together so that the air could not circulate around them. Some of those early November days could be quite warm and in the wrong conditions the birds could soon become quite 'high'. Once the birds had been cooled properly, however, they could be hung for anything up to two weeks and at the end of that time they were perfect for eating.

Shooting pheasants after he had raised them was not economically viable for the landowner. Each bird cost him overall £1 to raise, a cartridge cost 1s, and the bird as meat fetched 5s on the meat market. The saying was, therefore, 'Up goes £1, bang goes 3d, and down comes 2s 6d.' This came from a contemporary cartoon in *Punch*. Some people say that a pheasant is best when it has maggots in it but this is far from true. Once the maggots are in the carcase it must be disposed of. Flies must not be allowed near the carcases. Properly kept game-larders were fly-proof. In some places the game-larder was built outside and encased entirely in fly-proof netting so that there was still a free flow of air through the whole construction. At Benacre the larder was indoors but all windows and doorways had fly-proof netting.

Even the most junior keeper received a brace of pheasants at Christmas and mine were well received by my mother. The keepers themselves were given a hamper as their yuletide reward. In it was a turkey, a bottle of whisky, a bottle of port, a bottle of sherry, oranges and nuts.

The shoots continued over the Christmas period and there was always a shoot on Boxing Day. There have always been two types of keeper: the bloodthirsty character who keeps on putting up birds to be virtually slaughtered by the guns, and the other man who thinks more of his pheasants. If he thinks his birds are being slaughtered wholesale he does something about it. He might well hold back his line of beaters and use his dog to make the birds flush in great numbers over the guns so that not too many could possibly be hit. This could not be done too frequently, however, as the ploy would become too obvious. Perhaps the best method was when the keeper flushed his birds at a greater distance so that when they approached the guns they would fly too fast and too high to present easy targets.

Shooting pheasants, then, can be a convoluted business and in that first year at Benacre, even as a stop at the corner of a wood, by watching and listening to what was happening, I received an excellent grounding in the craft.

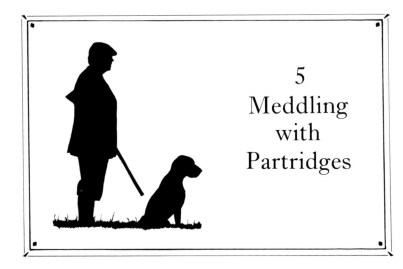

5
Meddling with Partridges

A wise sportsman knows that it is unwise to shoot partridges after the middle of December for in January the birds pair up and the most vital months are February and March when the partridge has difficulty finding food. At the end of the shooting period, there should be a good stock of birds left, hopefully sixty or seventy pairs, but winter wastage must be taken into account. This is not too serious in a mild winter but, no matter what the weather, some birds die every year. A keeper does not always find them for, like all dying creatures, they prefer to do so quietly, sometimes in rabbit holes and, at others, under tree roots. Far more birds are lost if there is a shortage of food, so the sensible keeper always takes food to his partridges in February and March. The best plan is to select sheltered places along the hedgerows and to put the seed where the partridges, and not wandering pheasants and woodpigeons, will find it. Pigeons would not go straight for it as they tend to feed more towards the centre of the field, avoiding hedgerows where predators might lurk. It was especially satisfying to see the partridges feasting on the food and, eventually, gathered and waiting for me to bring their daily rations. Sensible feeding during these two critical months reduces winter waste of birds considerably.

The next problem which reared its head as we tried to rear the partridges was vermin. The main objective of the partridge-keeper was to raise two birds where the previous year there had been one, and to achieve this aim pests had to be rigorously controlled. Then, as now, there was criticism of the measures that were taken, but a balance must be found and vermin of all sorts kept down. The keeper kept his job only as long as he achieved the results his employer wanted and this was often judged by his ability to eradicate pests.

To a good keeper pest-control presented little difficulty but a lot of work at the right time. When the crops were gathered in and the fields resultantly bare, the family, be it stoats, carrion crows, sparrow-hawks or foxes, breaks up. Food was now scarce for them as well as for the game birds. The stoat would wander many miles over the next three months. The sparrow-hawk could cover a score of miles in a morning, but winged vermin is more attached to its own locality than is its four-footed cousin.

At the first sign of spring, about the middle of March, the crows and foxes, weasels, stoats and sparrow-hawks pair up and settle in a place for the breeding season. This has always been the time to clear the beat of vermin and if it is done thoroughly the job can then be left until the following winter, unless, that is, the beat is surrounded by land where there are no such controls and the vermin comes in from outside as fast as it is removed.

I soon learned to recognise signs of vermin. A dead rabbit with its eyes pecked out was the work of a carrion or hooded crow. A bunch of feathers in a field used to clothe a fieldfare; they were too far away from the fence to be the work of a cat and, indeed, the unfortunate bird had fallen victim to a sparrow-hawk. Stoat tracks could be seen by the careful observer, frequently in the soft ground near a spring, and rats would haunt the fence near where the potatoes were hogged.

A light fall of snow at this period was a great help to the keeper. Tracks stood out distinctly even from a distance of 10yd. Every rat, stoat and weasel announced his presence on the beat and it was obvious that there were more pheasants than I had supposed in the big wood. Some of the rabbit burrows were

The hooded crow

not being used and I made a note to fill them in. Partridge tracks were to be seen everywhere, but we had to be careful not to over-estimate the number of birds for, being so hungry, they would cover more ground as they searched for food and it was easy to think you had more partridges than were actually there.

Absence of signs of vermin, while pleasing to the keeper, was also a warning to him because territory is like a vacuum. If not in use it will soon be claimed by a fresh pair of stoats or a couple of wandering carrion crows who may settle there at the end of March.

There were rats everywhere and the keeper had to rid his land of these thieves. They were around stack-yards, potato heaps and in sheltered burrows around the fields. As spring arrives they leave these areas and move into the hedgerows where they can be a great nuisance to partridge nests. On Benacre we began by putting down bait which included sugar and something aromatic to attract the rats. This had to be done, when possible, before they moved into the hedgerows. I went around all the places where rats were concentrated and carried with me a bag, holding about 5lb of bait, and a long bamboo pole with a spoon on the end. On finding a hole, I reached in with the implement and deposited some of the bait. This was done every day for four or five days and then the area was left alone for a few days to allow the rats to become thoroughly hungry. Then I would go around again, leaving the scented bait in the same places as before, but to the bait had been added a proportion of arsenic which was widely used in those days but which is now considered to be a cruel poison. After a few more days had elapsed I revisited the places that had been baited and found numerous dead rats, usually near puddles of water, which were collected and buried. It was important to make sure that there was no poison left in the holes.

The partridge's biggest enemy is the carrion crow, but an equal nuisance is the domestic cat which has gone wild. It is practically always a male and extremely difficult to catch because it is so unpredictable. It is also amazingly cunning and when we saw its tracks in the snow we had to do all we could to rid the beat of it at once. On the bare fields and in the leafless woods it was far easier to see and to trap than it would have been later.

Every farm had cats and a feral cat might sometimes live among them. If a rogue cat was disturbing our area, we would visit each farm and ask the tenant to keep his own cats inside on a fixed day, at which time we would go around his stack-yards and hay-lofts where the feral cat might be hiding. We would send in a terrier which, with a bit of luck, bolted the cat which was then shot. However, it was not always as easy as that. It might not have lived on the beat at all, but at the end of March when the fieldmice began to move and small birds to nest it would patrol fences every night. We would put down a few traps in such a way that the cat could reach the bait from either side of the fence or hedge but with only one means of access to the trap. The best bait was a good piece of smelly haddock, but we had to be cunning to cover the trap well both to hide it from the cat and to avoid small birds flying into it. Before setting such traps, the keeper would rub his hands on the ground and in the mud to reduce the amount of scent transferred to the trap. Another good bait is rancid bacon, but liver or young rabbit can also be used. The best bait of all was common valerian, a herb with pink or white flowers but with the most dreadful smell. To catch a cat the trap had to be well pegged down because a cat weighing nearly a stone, and in pain, can display great strength.

The quickest and surest way to rid the beat of a prowling cat is to take a short walk at dusk armed with a pair of binoculars and a gun. The glasses can cover a lot of ground and see where three or four fences meet. The cat would continue to hunt along fences in the hour before dusk. It was best not to relax this evening walk even when the days became longer as spring turned to summer and the partridge eggs were hatched. Young partridges rarely stray more than 50yd from the nest before they can fly.

Carrion crows are nasty creatures and no good keeper can afford to have even one on his beat. They will kill young birds, and young hares and rabbits, but their speciality is egg-hunting at which they are very clever. Fortunately, they are very easy to trap. My favourite method was to build a dummy nest at the end of March. This faced south-east and three egg-shells, left over from breakfast, were covered almost entirely with bracken or leaves. The nest was usually built under a gorse bush and had only one possible entrance; the shank of the jaws of the trap could be buried fairly deep and the plate about 9in from the nearest egg-shell. If the crow failed to go for the egg-shells the trap was baited with a small rabbit, but we were careful never to use the eggs of game birds because both pheasants and partridges are curious and the last thing we wanted was to trap a hen pheasant in search of a nesting site. When trapping failed, we looked for the crow's roost which was always where the bird had a wide view of the area, either in a tall tree or one at the edge of a copse. This has always presented the keeper with a difficulty because, even when sitting on her nest, the hen bird can see him coming and will leave the nest before she is shot.

Our best bet was to persevere and to try to get the cock bird, a restless beast and always on guard, who let out a raucous squawk if he saw us coming. This alerted the hen and off she flew. Sometimes we were rewarded in our hunt and sometimes we failed, but we had to try.

The sparrow-hawk was hunted and killed mercilessly at that time because with its immense wing-power it could cover great distances every day. It kills a pheasant or partridge chick out in the open rather than risk its precious wings and feathers in the top of a thick hedge in pursuit of a small bird. This hawk prefers to hunt along fences or small spinneys and a good way to bring it down was to drive a spinney while a gun stood at the end and shot it as it emerged. It was not an easy bird to trap as it loves to catch and kill its own food. The best trap was a small wicker case of linnets or chaffinches which was set out in the open; on top of it was a basket trap or it could be surrounded by ordinary Dorset traps, set into the ground. The linnets or chaffinches could easily be obtained using a few breadcrumbs and a small piece of garden netting raised on pegs which could be quickly withdrawn by an attached string. However, it was always easier to shoot the sparrow-hawk than to trap it. It nests in the second half of April and the hen could usually be shot as she left the nest, but it was important to kill the cock bird, too. He is only half the size of the hen but just as murderous. When we used the trap method we always released the small birds afterwards.

The damage done by kestrel hawks has long been the subject of heated discussion and it is now widely accepted that about 5 per cent of them will take game chicks. It was fascinating to watch an old kestrel hen in July teaching her young to range over the second crop of clover. By keeping an eye on the kestrels' nest we could soon see whether they were killing game birds by examining their pellets. If they were, their droppings would contain the remains of feet and feathers.

Both sparrow-hawk and kestrel take no less than forty-two days to incubate their eggs and nesting is a difficult time for them.

Of the other winged vermin the rook was and still is the least desirable. It was always too numerous, but reducing its numbers was difficult. Although the bird does not range over the ground deliberately looking for pheasant and partridge nests in the manner of the carrion crow, it will take the eggs if it sees them.

The magpie is smaller and less cunning than the rook and much easier to trap. The jay will occasionally take partridge eggs but prefers those of the thrush and the blackbird.

The brown owl, which destroys large numbers of young green plovers, is a bad character in the eyes of the keeper and was destroyed as he appeared. He will never pass a young pheasant or a partridge chick if he sees one. This owl's nest is quite easy to find but, even were it not, the bird has a perfectly regular beat along certain spinneys or fences and can readily be intercepted with a gun. The barn owl, on the other hand, is quite harmless.

As for stoats and weasels, they pair early in the spring when we would set up all of our tunnel traps. They had been cleaned out and made ready by the end of March. The stoats and weasels moved into the hedgerows and this was where they were caught. The traps could be made of wood shaped into tunnels about 3ft long or drainpipes could be used. These animals will investigate any chink or small hole they see and were therefore easy to trap once the fence or bank they frequented was found. The angle where three or four fences met was always a favourite place as was a sunny bank forming the southern boundary of a small wood or any bank where rabbits were numerous. Both stoats and weasels love to rub themselves against a gatepost.

94

The sparrow-hawk

Hawk trap as used in the twenties and thirties, and now an efficient jay trap

'Doctor Deadfall' trap

Various forms of box-traps and deadfall traps were used but the deadliest of all was the common Dorset trap. With them we would make a small shallow hole with sloping sides; this hole was about 2ft long and 6in wide. The trap was set into this hole and worked into the ground until the shank was a little below the ground surface while the plate was level with the surface. We then placed 2in drainpipes at each side of the trap so that one end of the pipe led directly onto the plate of the trap while the other led to the surface, thus forming a small underground run with the trap-plate at the central point. The sides were earthed in and a flat stone or turfs placed over the top before bracken was spread over the whole thing. Bait was not needed nor was it necessary to cover the plate although many keepers did so with moss or fine grass and leaves. Even if the trap were temporarily moved, the pipes remained untouched so that they could be used at a later date.

Much less elaborate traps could be used to great advantage and a single trap guarded by a covered pipe high by the side of a gatepost or a gap in a fence usually accounted for a passing weasel; in fact, any position where the animal had to run through a chink or down a small hole was a good place for a trap.

A young rabbit, which can be found lying dead almost any day in April or May, could be used as bait by being lodged under an overhanging bank and guarded by two well-sunken traps; this would always account for some blood-feeding vermin on the shoot. Old traps were nearly always used, but if new ones were used, they were buried underground for a month or so to remove any smell which would be alien to their intended victim.

If you mention the hedgehog to most people you conjure up a picture of Beatrix Potter's Mrs Tiggywinkle with her mop cap and white apron, or a little creature shuffling along a country path. To the keeper, however, the hedgehog is an offensive little beast and it is difficult to find a good word to say in its favour. It has an unpleasant habit of walking round and round a sitting bird and just brushing it with its spikes; neither pheasant nor partridge will suffer this harassment for long. The hedgehog's mouth is too small to do any damage to a pheasant's egg and only rarely can it break it at the pointed end, but the will to do so is there and when unbroken eggs were found rolled out of their nest it was usually certain that it was the hedgehog's work. Our terriers were expert at finding hedgehogs and a dusk stroll, 'all in the April evening', always resulted in the dogs finding several, especially in clover or in good pasture. Even without a dog the keeper could always find hedgehogs for they have well-defined runs usually parallel to a hedge and very near to it. Many also found their way into tunnel traps. Many keepers believed that a dead hedgehog suspended against the trunk of a tree, about 1ft from the ground, would attract all the hedgehogs in the immediate area and so a trap would be placed just below the dead hedgehog. From the fact that many hedgehogs were trapped in this way we must assume that there was some sense in the old theory, although why this should be so is unknown.

It would be childish to pretend that the fox is not a dangerous nuisance in partridge country and if there is no meet of foxhounds within 10 or 12 miles, then it is simply foolish to preserve foxes. If in February or March, long before cubs are born, the keeper comes across a new earth being opened he can be almost 100 per cent certain that it is intended for a new litter. In these circumstances he would dress it with paraffin and dig it in, thus driving the foxes away from that immediate area, an essential act if the projected earth was near the partridge beat. If foxes were running the hedges during the partridge breeding season, the keeper was well advised to lose a few nests deliberately. Some authorities advocated dressing the hedge and bank on each side of the nest with a patent dressing, a repellent, or the nest itself could be dressed. In Suffolk the method we used was very diffferent. As soon as one of our keepers found a partridge nest he put down a dead rabbit, a rat or a handful of bullock's lights, or anything which would become carrion in three or four weeks. This was placed in the grass or young corn about 9ft from the nest and on the lee side of the fence since the prevailing wind is usually steady in May. The bait did not become really offensive until the partridge had begun to sit and, in any case, it would not drive her away. The prowling fox might have come either way along the fence but, as ever, he used his nose to the best advantage and located the carrion long before he found the nest. He was unlikely to eat the rotten flesh but foxes love to roll on it, as do many dogs, and there was a good chance that he would be sufficiently distracted to miss the nest and the smell of the carrion usually meant that he did not get wind of the partridge. This remedy is not infallible but it has been established practice for much longer than my fifty years in the business. The sitting partridge is in the greatest danger from the fox just when her eggs are hatching, probably because the eggs give off a strong game smell of gas as they hatch. Added to that the hen partridge becomes restless and fidgety at this time and also gives off a strong game scent as she moves about or fluffs up her feathers.

By far the most important part of partridge preservation is the prevention of inbreeding. If a covey or eleven of twelve young partridges remains together until it is time for them to pair there will be two or three pairs inbreeding in the most undesirable way. Even if two superfluous hens pair into a covey in the adjoining field the chances are that there is still a close relationship, and this must also be prevented. The introduction of new blood from time to time is absolutely essential and the advantage of this is so obvious that the interchange of eggs from various parts of the country has become established practice; many thousand Hungarian partridges have been imported for the same reason.

At about the beginning of this century the Euston system was invented, so called because it was first tried on a large scale on the Duke of Grafton's estate, Euston, in Suffolk. It simply consists of taking up the eggs of game birds as fast as they are laid and substituting pot eggs in their place. The partridge will sit on pot eggs while the real eggs are put in an incubator or under a hen. When a clutch of the real eggs began to chip we would take them in a flannel-lined basket to the nest of a bird which had been sitting for no less than two weeks. These we put under the partridge in place of the pot eggs. It was childishly simple and the partridge took kindly to the pot eggs on which she would happily sit for the full incubation period of twenty-four days. There was almost no danger of the bird deserting her nest as long as she was removed quietly from the nest and had been sitting for between fourteen and eighteen days. A partridge lifted from her nest will be back on it within a few minutes of the time you leave it.

The possibilities of the Euston system are endless. The eggs of all the native birds can be mixed at will and the eggs received from a Hampshire friend can be placed in any nest. If a pheasant had reason to suspect that there was something wrong with her nest she would probably desert it.

If a prowling cat kills a partridge on her nest, the use of the Euston system means that the eggs will still be safe and, as long as sufficient trouble is taken, the rook and carrion crow will have to look elsewhere for game bird eggs. It always amused me to watch a rook as it puts its head on one side to contemplate a pot egg, having tried unsuccessfully to puncture it with its beak. These artificial eggs can be bought from dealers in game bird equipment and are so well made that the casual observer could not tell the difference.

We made our preparations for the breeding season so that all was ready by the middle of April. A good keeper was always prepared to look after up to fifty partridge nests on his beat.

The really serious business of partridge-rearing began about the first week in May as the birds always seem to consistently lay their eggs around 8 May. On 10 May 1936, I took a long walk around the beat and found eleven nests with different numbers of eggs and these were marked on a plan of the beat which I had previously drawn showing spinneys, footpaths, hedgerows and fields with their names. The marking of these nests onto the chart was done with meticulous care, giving distances from such landmarks as 'the big holly bush' or 'the pond'. Each nest was given an initial, A, B, C, and so on, and, as the eggs were collected, they were marked with the initial of the nest from which they were taken. Also on the plan I wrote the date on which the first egg was laid in each nest. Partridges do not lay regularly every day but do so sporadically until they have accumulated seven or eight eggs. As we gradually collected the eggs we kept them on trays in rows, those from each nest occupying their own row. When an exchange had been agreed with a keeper in another part of England, the head keeper selected forty eggs from a dozen different nests with a view to changing as much blood as possible. These eggs were then packed tightly in bran or fine sawdust in a stout tin box and sent off to their destination.

By this time we were beginning to make up clutches of about eighteen eggs selected from as many nests as possible. As more and more nests were discovered and the birds were laying freely, it became possible to make up clutches in such a way that each egg was from a different nest. A partridge only begins to feather her nest on the day she lays her last egg but one, and when she lays the last egg she uncovers all of her eggs and leaves them uncovered until she begins to sit at nightfall that day. On paper this may sound a very complicated procedure, but in practice it is exceedingly simple, as long as the plan is always faithfully marked up. The rewards of this system, seen two seasons later, are so great that they can only be appreciated when seen, and the chances of inbreeding are virtually eliminated.

As soon as a clutch was made up it was placed under a hen or in an incubator; in those days most keepers went in for batteries of bantams as they did not trust an incubator and very few of them were remotely mechanically minded. A smoky incubator would have been a great worry to them. Like the pheasant's egg, that of the partridge takes twenty-four days to incubate, but a close-sitting hen or an incubator does the job in twenty-three days, being just a fraction warmer. On about the twenty-second day of the incubation period, each clutch was carefully examined and when four or five of the eggs had begun to chip they were placed under the first partridge which had begun to sit, whichever bird the plan showed that to have been. Should one or two of the chicks have already hatched they could still be placed in the nest with the other eggs without the partridge minding at all. We had done all we could at that point, apart from keeping a watchful eye open for a rambling cat in the long June and July evenings, and had no further partridge-rearing tasks until the following January. That, at least, was our hope. Almost all the nests had been found and those that were very well concealed were left alone, save that the eggs in them were removed and replaced by other assorted real ones. There was no need for pot eggs to be used there.

Clutches of eggs hatched daily and it was then that the importance of the dates on the plan became evident. Eggs were never put under a partridge until she had been sitting for at least sixteen days. The eggs from Yorkshire used to present us with something of a problem as they were of great value; a particularly well hidden and almost inaccessible nest was chosen and into it went a clutch of eighteen eggs from the north just a few hours before they hatched. In such a difficult spot it was unlikely that any of these would be shot during the season. The

Shooting party on a grouse moor, showing head keeper's fell pony

A shooting party of guns and beaters by a watcher's house on a grouse moor

remaining imported eggs were divided and placed in nests where we could keep an eye on the chicks when they hatched or where birds had been rather scarce in previous years.

By the end of June our work in this respect was almost done; most of the nests had hatched and the birds disappeared into the various crops.

As soon as the partridge brood is fairly strong on the wing, the birds can take care of themselves reasonably well. Supervised by their parents they will cover quite an area in a particular field. Towards the last light of the day they can be seen to take to the wing and to fly to the centre of the field where they adopt an all-round defence and leave no scent. Thus no predator can find them by their scent alone.

Some of my colleagues were invited to accompany their employers to the north of England for a few days of grouse-shooting in August. There they acted as loaders for the employer and also as his valet. They all enjoyed this as it was a complete change of scene and the northern fells are at their best at that time of year. It was interesting to talk to the other keepers and to discuss differences in their work and when they came south again they had many tales to tell us. They had seen how grouse were shot and were eager to tell how, when it came to perks and gratuities, the tips given by the guns to the keepers were about three times as much as they might have expected at the end of a week's partridge shooting. People did and do travel from all over the world to shoot grouse in the north of England for they make remarkably good shooting. The lads who had made the journey north all noticed the extra strain on their leg muscles while walking the fells, but they all regarded the trip as a holiday and looked forward eagerly to the first partridge shoot which was usually in the second week of September.

There was and always will be something very rewarding about rearing partridges and watching them grow to maturity.

6
Molies and Conies and Long-legged Beasties

Almost since man's first appearance on earth there have been folk tales about animals. Much of this lore appeared in Aesop's fables, and I heard much of it as a boy and a young keeper.

One of my favourite creatures, although it can be a nuisance, is the hare. It usually mates in March and most people have heard of mad March hares. I have often been lucky enough to see them boxing; two males stand on their hind legs and punch at each other, having literally come to blows over a female. The female can have several litters of leverets during the summer; her gestation period is a matter for debate since there are those who hold it to be six weeks while others think it to be a month. Personally, I have always believed the old saying that 'the hare and the mare both take a year'. The mare takes forty-eight weeks and the meaning of the old saying is that the hare, therefore, takes forty-eight days. Unlike the rabbit, which bears its young underground, the female hare makes a form which is a nest in some kind of cover, usually where it is dry. There she has her young, usually three or four, and, whereas the baby rabbit is born naked, the leveret is born with a coat of greyish fur. Nor are they blind at birth and all in all they are delightful little creatures. Their most attractive features are their extremely long ears and sparkling blue eyes. They can be picked up by humans and display no fear at all. They grow rapidly and it is the three-quarter grown animals frequently seen at harvest time which are supposed to be so good for the table.

East Anglia, in particular, had a great deal of folklore about the hare. The older people contended that the hare was associated with witches who could, it was believed, take the form of a hare. This belief arose from the idea that the hare, being so swift, would be the quickest way of escaping from the burning stake. Not only is it swift, it is also supremely graceful and can certainly give even the best dogs, including lurchers and greyhounds, more than a run for their money. All of this refers to the brown or common hare and not the mountain hare.

Country people used to swear that the hare could change sex at will and do so as frequently as once a month while others held that it could only do so once a year. These ideas must have had their origin in some old happening which had been corrupted in repeated tellings. It also used to be said, and firmly believed, that at certain times of the year a hare could be killed only by the use of a silver bullet, but there were precious few of those in Covehithe, or in the whole of Suffolk. Silver bullets are associated, in horror stories at least, with vampires and the supernatural, but why the hare should be linked with these things is a mystery in itself. As far as the keeper was concerned, killing a hare was a most distasteful job.

Farmers, however, hate hares as do foresters. In winter, when everything has a covering of snow, the leader of a small conifer sticking up from the snow is a tempting bite for the hare. No wonder that foresters become angry because once the leader has been nipped off the tree it will no longer grow normally. However the hare never eats this part of the tree once it has been removed, so it really is nothing but an act of vandalism. Farmers have always argued that two hares will eat as much grass as a sheep and in years when there is a large hare population, farmers become very angry as they watch their precious crops dwindle. Many people forget that grass is a very expensive crop and that grazing land is at a premium.

On Benacre it was the keepers' job to cull the hares to reduce their population and on hare drives it was possible to see

106

pastures absolutely moving with hares. Up to two hundred guns would be used to cover huge areas of land and hundreds of hares were driven towards the guns. In Suffolk that method was not used but many hares were shot on partridge days and others in the woodland on shoot days. The hare drives described here were on another estate, long after I had left Benacre, and used to sicken me because the hares ran along in front of the walking guns. They knew full well their fate and as they were driven towards the standing guns they would sit up on their back legs and cry like babies, a heart-rending sound. Shooting hares was detestable, but it had to be done. Some hardened guns would turn away from the sight and slip their gun into its sleeve. Such vast culls are no longer necessary since the animals do not exist in the large numbers we saw in the thirties or, in fact, as recently as the fifties. How much their demise is related to modern farming methods and weed-killers one cannot say for certain but real concern is at last being voiced as to why the hare population has gone into such a steep decline. Poachers have always pursued hares but the blame cannot be laid at their door alone. Beagle packs hunt hares today and did so when I was a lad in Suffolk, although not at Benacre where the game bird rearing was so intensive.

Rabbits, however, we did have, and in abundance. They can breed at six months old and the gestation period is just twenty-eight days. A doe can have six litters a year with five to seven young in each litter. Many employers have remarked how 'that damned keeper has been working on rabbits all winter and there are as many now as when he started'. Very few landowners seem to understand how rapidly rabbits can breed. Keepers do their best to reduce the population, but try to imagine the phenomenal numbers there would be without such measures. For centuries rabbits were born underground in burrows or warrens, but since myxomatosis they can now be found in nests in hedgerows and dense cover on top of the ground. It has to be somewhere warm because they are born without any coat at all. Those born above ground are also more vulnerable to predation. In the wild today there are rabbits of all colours, black, white, blue and the common brown, a situation brought about by tame rabbits having escaped and bred in the countryside. Rabbits, although very timid, are strong in defence of their young. Their natural enemies are the stoats and weasels and I have seen a doe rabbit attack a weasel which ventured near her nest. She was soon joined by two other does which quickly put the weasel to flight and pursued it for quite a distance. Even stoats, which are bigger than weasels, have been seen off in the same way. The paradox is that, apart from at breeding times, a rabbit confronted by a stoat or weasel just gives up, squeals and allows its attacker to kill it. Normally, a rabbit does not bite unless you try to touch the young ones, and many warreners have been bitten by an adult rabbit as they have tried to pull out its offspring. A rabbit's teeth are both long and sharp and can inflict a nasty wound, but the rabbit's best-known defensive tactic is the sort of karate chop it can deliver with its back feet. Buck rabbits can be seen to rush at each other and then turn to lash out with these strong back feet. Such behaviour is usually seen at mating times.

The keeper has always had to make every effort to keep the rabbit population down and many have lost their jobs for failing to do so effectively. At Benacre, once the pheasant shooting was over, we had only a month to ferret the rabbits. We used ferrets then because, as a rule, no young rabbits had yet been born, the first coming in late February, and the animals we caught were good and clean and suitable for sale.

There were far more rabbits between the wars than there are today, and at Benacre, as elsewhere, all the fields had to be netted in completely or the crops would have been completely destroyed. The rabbits ate everything and anything and would take a field of corn down to stubble. They acted as devastatingly on grassland so that there was not enough pasture even for sheep. Also, whereas hares are clean creatures in their habits, rabbits are the opposite. They foul their own burrows which are covered in flies in summer. They are also always flea-infested.

The mole is the hero of numerous children's stories but is, in reality, a pest. It seems to me that there are far more now than when I was young because in days gone by farmers kept on top of the problem. Today, mole-catchers are employed but previously farmers did the job themselves. They did so with traps as we did, and the occasional few shillings could be made from selling moleskins for which there was a heavy demand. They were used for workmen's trousers in the main. There is an art in catching moles in traps. You have to find the main runs for when a mole is searching for food he pushes up the soil and makes molehills. He makes a tunnel but has then to remove the soil he has displaced, thus creating the molehills. Worms, making their way through the soil, wriggle into his tunnel and when the mole next passes that way he usually finds the worm which he eats. This is his feeding ground and the runs which lead to it are shallow. Traps were set in the main tunnel, this having been found with a probe. The traps were made in such a way that the jaws were open once it was set; it had a round trigger with a small hole in it and this was placed in the dead centre of the run. As the mole came along the run, he tried to push through but succeeded only in activating the jaws which then trapped him. The initial placing of the trap was accomplished by the digging of a small hole with a trowel; the hole was shaped, great care being taken that there was no soil in the run on either side of the trap which was dropped in. The soil was then pressed down over the trap. There was a knack to this job but it was soon learned by trial and error.

Moles can destroy a complete pasture by undermining it and pushing up molehills and the best way to be rid of them is to poison them with strychnine. A licence to purchase the poison must be obtained from the ministry; this is then taken to the chemist, who dispenses the poison. Then several hundred worms are collected while a farmer is ploughing and these are placed in a large tin containing soil. A few worms at a time are placed on a sacking of loose weave. These wriggle through the sacking which makes them clean. A little strychnine is sprinkled over them to kill them. Using a long pair of tweasers and wearing surgical gloves, the treated worms are placed in a tin from where they are pushed into the mole runs, just where the mole would expect to find them. He then eats the poisoned worms and dies. Properly used, this method can clear an area of moles completely. This is, incidentally, the only purpose for which strychnine will be dispensed.

The moleskins were sold to Horace Friend who took just about any pelts, except rabbit, but there was even an outlet for them to the skin and bone man who came to the area once a week and bought rabbit skins.

We tried to take a pair of rabbits to each cottager once a week as it helped their budget and, in return, they passed on information to us. In those days a poacher could not travel very far without being seen by somebody and the cottagers quickly passed word to the keeper if they saw something suspicious. Today, many people simply turn a blind eye to such happenings. A favourite Suffolk dish was rabbit pie which we liked to have cold for breakfast on Sunday. Also in the pie were pieces of salt pork and plenty of sage from the garden.

Some of the money made from the sale of pelts was put away to save up for a pair of 'Scotch boots' made by the Hogg family of Fife. They were of horse-hide and cost about 25s; they are still available today, but at over £80 a pair. I no longer wear them simply because they are too heavy.

When I took over the beat during Friday Thrower's illness, Sir Robert gave me a bonus of £10. Half of it was saved but with the rest I bought in Lowestoft a pair of Wellington boots, a new cap and, best of all, a mackintosh that really kept the rain out.

While Friday was ill, little Billy, as we knew him, another beat-keeper, used to pedal over to see how I was managing. He did not have too many birds to look after and so would arrive at about 5.45 in the morning from his home 4 miles away. His greatest concern was that Friday might be worried that I had slept in and he suggested that on arriving each morning I should bang the side of my hut a few times with a big stick. Friday, he said, would hear this and rest easy in his bed. I adopted that practice, therefore, and he did hear me, too often perhaps, as my rather enthusiastic banging may have told more people than Friday that Boy Johnny had arrived and was on the beat.

A familiar creature on the Benacre beat was the grey squirrel, a pest of the first order and not just to the gamekeeper. The forester had no love for him either. It takes the eggs of game birds and frequently destroys their nests. The animal is a native of the hardwood forests of North America and was introduced into this country in the mid-nineteenth century. It was at the start of the twentieth century that it became established in the wild here. Now it can live happily in parkland, trees of the hedgerow and gardens and does not necessarily need large areas of trees as a habitat. There has long been a school of thought which contends that the grey squirrel is not particularly aggressive towards its red cousin, but there is incontrovertible proof to suggest the opposite. Grey squirrels attack red and the grey has definitely replaced the red in most places. As well as feeding on nuts, acorns and fungi, grey squirrels also eat tree bark, leaves, shoots, buds and flowers and in commercial woodlands they are more than just a nuisance. Strangely enough, the grey squirrel has very few enemies and can live for up to ten years. Their mating season is from April to June and it is then that they do the most damage for in their frustration they scratch at the bark of, particularly, hardwood trees and will strip them all the way round. At that time of year the bark is particularly soft and is easily stripped. Trying to control grey squirrels is almost a pointless exercise for keepers because the area he does manage to clear becomes a vacuum which almost immediately fills up with more grey squirrels.

In 1935 there was an abundance of grey squirrels throughout East Suffolk but there were plenty of red ones, too. The red squirrel is a very endearing creature. He is much smaller than the grey and works very hard collecting acorns, beech mast and other food. Friday called them 'pudden-headed' because they bury their hoards of food in various places and then forget where they have done so. The result is that in a very short time the acorns and nuts start to grow. Young trees spring up all over the place and the red squirrel is the inadvertent forester who creates this new growth; he is the Johnny Appleseed of the English countryside. The grey squirrel, on the other hand,

takes its food up to its home, the dray, an unmistakable construction of twigs built high in a tree. It will also nest in holes in
mature trees. Most squirrel activity takes place in daylight and,
despite what we all learned at school about squirrels hibernating
in the winter, they can still be seen foraging in all but the most
severe winter months.

Grey squirrels inhabited all the southern counties of England
up as far as the Humber and they have gradually moved north-
ward. They are now so widely and densely spread that the
authorities are becoming very worried about them and the
serious threat they present to woodlands.

At Benacre we caught hundreds of grey squirrels in tunnel
traps but this was not deliberate and at that time we did not class
them as a nuisance, mainly because our woodland was com-
posed of mature trees which they did not damage. We did know
that they would take pheasants eggs and therefore shed no tears
when they were caught.

Red squirrels are best seen just after dawn, Scots pine planta-
tions being one of the best places to look for them. I was once
told that the Scots pine was the only large native conifer to survive the last Ice Age and that the red squirrel was one of the last
mammals to colonise Britain before it was cut off by the North
Sea from the rest of Europe about nine thousand years ago.

In North America grey squirrels are eaten in a pie but I have
never, fortunately, been that hungry.

Another occasional nuisance at Benacre was the coypu, introduced into this country from South America to be raised in
cages for its pelt. That was in 1929 and, inevitably, some soon
escaped and began to breed in the wild. They do eat some crops
but their most annoying habit is the way they tunnel into river
and canal banks, eventually causing them to collapse. To look
at, the coypu is a sort of overgrown rat, and used to turn up
occasionally in our tunnel traps.

We never bothered to skin squirrels and coypu. We would
have been able to sell them but preferred to avoid such sidelines
and to make our wages stretch as far as we could.

Mother was paid about half of my money for my keep and

Southwold Road, Wrentham

some of the rest I saved. Part of these savings went towards paying for my annual new suit. For this stylish outfit I always went to Burtons in Lowestoft. The trousers had 22in bottoms, the waistcoat was double-breasted and the jacket was short as was the fashion. The suit was always navy-blue serge and made to measure. This masterpiece of sartorial elegance, which arrived two weeks later, cost 30s, but I felt like a man of the world when I put it on.

I was always accompanied on the annual tailoring expedition by my great friend, Jack Girling, who ordered his suit at the same time. He lived in Wrentham and worked at a brick kiln. He had been in the class above me at school and we became firm friends later. We spent much of our free time together, usually at the Five Bells on the outskirts of Wrentham, but we only went there when we had spare money, which was not very often. In bad winters we walked over hedges to the pub, so deep was the snow. There was nothing pretentious about the Five Bells but it was very cosy. We used to play darts and exchange news and gossip. The landlord was Alec Briggs and he had a lovely old car, an Hispano Suiza, in which he sometimes ran us into Lowestoft. It was the first car I really knew, a convertible

113

with a wide running board, great power, and enormous round headlights covered by a grid.

Jack and I used the saloon bar of the pub in which there was a piano. Most evenings ended with a sing-song around it, and a few girls usually turned up. We would occasionally take a couple out for the evening but we did not court seriously.

The Five Bells was definitely the place to be on Christmas Eve. It was not the sort of celebration you see in pubs today. There was little in the way of food except for pickled eggs and we kept ourselves warm by drinking pints of old and mild into which had been plunged a red-hot poker.

Winter was the slackest time for a keeper and when we drank late into the night I could have stayed in bed until 7 o'clock or later the following morning, but, although I rolled home on more than one occasion I never slept in. I had to do the odd nightwatch but there was little poaching then of the type we see today. Nobody ever entered the cover where there were a lot of birds, but the occasional pheasant did disappear from the edge of the estate, usually taken by a farm labourer. This petty poaching never got out of hand on Benacre.

Sometimes during the winter months I cycled to the cinema in Southwold. There were two performances each evening. I did not enjoy *The Good Earth,* a long-drawn-out film, but it was a different matter with *The Outlaw.* Jane Russell could have had my heart any time she wanted. It was the first sexy film I had ever seen.

A Saturday afternoon was the time we sometimes went all the way to Lowestoft by bus. The cinema there was the Odeon; it was luxurious and we could even have tea there before going in to see the film. Sandwiches and cakes before the show were always followed by fish and chips after it. The last bus back was at 11 o'clock, but it went only to Wrentham and I had to walk from there to Covehithe. If ever we missed the bus back, we faced a walk of 8 miles, but that was no hardship.

Buck Jones and Ken Maynard starred in more of the films I saw at the Odeon than anyone else. They had the fastest draw I had ever seen.

My favourite cinema, though, was that at Southwold because I occasionally went out with an usherette called Vera Gerald who worked there. She used to sneak me in at the back after the lights had been dimmed so that I did not have to pay. She put me in the expensive seats and when she had finished showing people to their places she came and sat with me. Sometimes we even had an ice cream. The cinema owner knew of our nocturnal liaison and turned a blind eye as I slipped in. I first met Vera on the Southwold promenade when I was wearing my navy-blue suit, one Sunday evening.

There was a large common in Southwold and an organisation called the Duke of York's Boys used to camp there. There was also a music hall and a theatre in Lowestoft where the acting company of J. B. Priestley performed. I preferred the music hall, probably because I found the pretty chorus girls very entertaining.

We had entertainment closer to home in the form of the weekly Saturday night dance in Wrentham, the music being supplied by the local town band led by the postman, Billy Chatfield. He played the tuba and when he did so his cheeks filled up like balloons. This was the same band which played around the farms at Christmas time, sometimes frightening the horses to such an extent that some of them broke loose and their owners spent half the night trying to bring them back.

We certainly worked hard on the estate but life had its lighter moments, too.

7

A Profusion
of Partridges

One of the Benacre traditions was that the first partridge shoot took place in the second week of September. There was none of the glamour that attaches to the Glorious Twelfth of the previous month which heralds in the grouse nor was there an influx of foreign visitors to shoot the partridge. They preferred shooting grouse, but the partridge possessed just as much magic for a lowland keeper.

I felt rather smug going out at first light onto my 'manor' and hearing and seeing the fruits of our year's work. The coveys were calling and chattering in that patchwork pattern of crops in the small fields with their neatly trimmed hedges. On the previous day Mr Herbert and I had gone over the ground we were going to shoot so that we could plan the drives. We took special note of the wind and trusted that it would be in the same direction the next day. The prevailing wind at that time of year is usually from the south-west, changed only on occasion by a period of rough, low-pressure weather. Usually, in September, the weather pattern is fairly settled and we could plan the drives accordingly, but we always had an alternative plan in case the wind changed or blew too strongly. Partridges must always be driven downwind at the start of the day, so the plan was to start the early drives downwind and to take all the birds from that corner of the beat and for the first four or five drives downwind.

The reason for this strategy is that partridges detest being driven away from their home territory anyway and to try to drive them into the wind would be most difficult. The four, or even five, afternoon drives would be into the wind because the partridges which have been driven from their homes in the morning will try hard and battle against the wind to return there.

Occasionally, the wind does change overnight but to change the drives at that stage is very difficult and can cause problems. There are those who say that once a plan has been made it should not be altered but driving birds into the wind at the start of the day can lead to nothing short of disaster. The wind has always to be considered very carefully when driving partridge.

Once our plan had been made, Mr Herbert explained the drives to our employer and to everyone else who was going to be involved in the shoot. Inadequate briefing can result in the guns going off in one direction while the beaters pursue quite the opposite course.

Transport had to be laid on and the game-carts readied, made clean and presentable. The beaters and pickers-up were told when and where to meet. On shooting day the beat-keeper met all the beaters, gave them their instructions and made sure that each man had a flag, a stick with a piece of white cloth at its end. Three or four of the men needed red flags for these were the flankers; they usually travelled with the guns and were under the command of the head keeper. They had to be intelligent because this was an important job; they stood at each end of the line of guns, the idea being that the flankers with their red flags would turn the partridges if they saw them breaking out at the end of the line of guns. It is a well-known fact that a partridge can be turned if it sees a flag within the first 10yd of its flight; after that, nothing will stop it. The flanker must be extremely alert, therefore, and when he sees that a covey has sprung into the air and appears to be veering off to one side or the other of the line of guns he must immediately stand up and show his flag. If he does this at the very start of the flight then he will be able to turn the birds. Grouse can be turned at almost any point in their flight but not the determined partridge. A bad flanker who does not keep his wits about him can easily spoil the whole day.

Mr Herbert placed the flankers, and I, as the beat-keeper, took the rest of the beaters and lined them up ready for the first drive. The tone of the partridge chatter now changed to one of alarm because of the unusual disturbance. At each end of the line stood a man with a red flag and usually two more in the middle of the line so that it could be seen quickly at any time during the drive. Beaters were spaced out so that on stubbles or grass they were about a 100yd apart, while on root fields they were closed up to about 50yd since it is more difficult to make partridges spring from thick cover like turnips, kale or rape. It is also very difficult to flush partridges from sugar-beet, although if there is a field of this directly in front of the guns and three or four coveys live there, then as the beaters come through the birds get up in twos or singly. As they fly over the guns this makes for successful sport and good shots could be achieved when this situation arose.

If, when the whistle was blown and the drive begun, it was seen that there was a fairly stiff cross-wind, the line was adjusted so that the beaters were further down on the windward side. This was because partridges have a natural tendency to go with the wind and this was counteracted by sending the appropriate wing of the line down on one side showing their flags while upwind only one beater was required. He could travel forward steadily as there was little fear of the birds breaking out upwind.

On the day of the shoot, the guns used to meet at the hall where they were all introduced to Mr Herbert. He could always tell which were the new guns out for their first shoot as they looked nervous and uncomfortable in their new shooting suits. These can be the most irritating clothes when they are new and it can take a lifetime to get used to wearing plus-twos and stockings. These trousers buckle at the knee and long stockings from the knee down are worn with them. The sight of a new boy, not yet used to the ways of these stockings which work their way down, showing half his calf, caused amusement. The more experienced wear garters but these must not be too tight as they can soon give rise to aching legs. The nervousness of the new

Thomas Horsley (Coney Street, York) Patent no 374 drop-down-barrel, breech-loading action shotgun, 1862, showing cams on hammers for resetting firing pins

guns was increased by the fact that they felt that they were being carefully observed and they must have sent up many a silent prayer that not too many birds would come over them.

The rest of the guns drew lots for the place where they would stand, as was done for pheasant shooting, in other words he who was number one for the first drive became number three for the second, and so on.

This having been established, all the guns climbed aboard the gun bus and drove off followed by the game-cart. This differed from that used for pheasants in that it was covered and had lines of hooks as it is important that partridges are hung onto hooks as soon as possible. On a warm September day they could, otherwise, quickly overheat and go off. The cart was also fitted with fly-proof muslin.

Having arrived at the first stand, the guns would check that all was well with their loaders and they were led to their places by Mr Herbert. When he was satisfied that all was as it should be, he gave several blasts on his whistle to start the drive. Soon there was a whirring of wings as the first cock birds flew across. The cracks of the first few shots rarely brought down any birds for these first birds were the old ones which are always stronger than the rest of the covey. This is not the case by October when the young birds are a little older and a lot stronger, perhaps even being in front of the old birds.

It is always pleasing to see covey after covey coming over the guns and, after the first shot, the birds scattering and going in all directions, providing excellent sport. Mr Herbert was expert at watching the direction taken by the birds missed by the guns. This he needed to know for the return drives later in the day.

The beat-keeper could be compared to a platoon sergeant, his beaters being, in this case, his platoon. I always tried to make sure that the men knew me and understood the signs I made to them. A bad-tempered keeper in charge of the beaters was disastrous because if he started to shout, things soon went wrong. Beaters do have to be checked sometimes, perhaps if one walks ahead of the rest or lags behind, because, if there is a gap in the line, the partridges quickly take advantage and will not go in the desired direction. Checking a beater can always be done pleasantly because although nobody likes being corrected, they hate having it done in front of others. Country folk, in particular, do not like to be singled out in this or any other way. At all events, one correction should suffice.

The birds could also be recalcitrant and there were always a few which would spring back over the beaters' heads; others would break out to the right or left. There is an art in driving which is acquired through experience and is the road to success in partridge-shooting.

By the end of the first drive the new guns had lost their nervousness and there would be about twenty brace in the bag. The end of the drive was signalled by a long whistle blast from Mr Herbert which let the guns know that the drive was finished. The guns were then handed over to the loaders to be put into their sleeves and I called the beaters to me and led them off to the next drive. The guns moved off to the next stand, in the guns' carriage if it were a distance away and on foot if it were near. The pickers-up had collected all the birds and taken them to the game-cart where they were hung at once under the beak. By lunchtime we usually had over a hundred brace.

Lunch was taken by the guns in the orchard and it was a splendid affair. The beaters took advantage of the break to have a rest and remove their boots for they had done a great deal of walking. For beating, the heaviest boots are the most comfortable.

After lunch all would be resumed again. The odd pheasant would rise as the beaters advanced but they could not be shot, nor would any ground game which had been flushed as to shoot towards the beaters at a low angle is a dangerous practice. Some pigeons might be shot.

By the late thirties there were pneumatic tyres on tumbrels but we always referred to them as wind tyres. These made life a lot easier for the horses. I was once told, as a lad when I helped on the farm, to take some feed to the shepherd, called George. At the time, he happened to have his flock in a turnip field. This was in the days when shepherds had portable huts on wheels, a feature familiar to readers of Thomas Hardy's *Far from the Madding Crowd,* and I had been asked to move the hut while I was at the field. The farm foreman had told me to use a horse called Linda who was in the stable. Linda was what used to be described as 'fizzy'; she was always left behind because if there was trouble to be found, she would be in the middle of it. Somewhat hesitantly I put Linda into the shafts of the tumbrel, loaded the sheep fodder into the back and went off. Going away from the farm it was very difficult to persuade Linda to move at all; she would continually stop and look back, but on a return journey there was no stopping her. I eventually arrived at the turnip field and saw that the roadway was between a narrow lane of hurdles, used in those days to contain the sheep. I was having some difficulty in steering Linda who was by now moving at a rapid pace. The turn into the lane of hurdles was rather sharp and, as I pulled round, one of the wide wind tyres hit the end of the hurdle and climbed up it. The tumbrel went over on its side, Linda fell onto her side and there was fodder everywhere. I had

Manpower in the fields

jumped clear but Linda was in a panic, fastened in the shafts and kicking violently. One of the shafts had broken but had not injured her, and George came running over. He, unfortunately, was in a bigger flap than I, and obviously did not relish the company of horses. I remembered being told that in a situation like this you should sit on the horse's head, and so I did. I asked George to unharness the animal and to give him his due, he did try, but was shaking so badly that he was physically incapable of doing so. I therefore asked if he would be good enough to come and sit on her head so that I could unhitch her. He protested in reply that he could not possibly allow me to do such a thing, but I could see that he was terrified of the very idea of sitting on a horse's head or even of being near one. At last, he unfastened the straps and chains and I rose gingerly from my unusual seat.

Linda jumped to her feet and shook herself but she was in a
nervous state, prancing and sweating. I surveyed the cart and
rapidly concluded that I could not return it to the farm, nor
could I move the hut and I could certainly not ride Linda in her
agitated state. My only course was to lead her back, which I did,
but with great difficulty. When we returned, I met the foreman,
Mouldy Keeble, who said drily, 'I see you've been in trouble. I
don't know what the agent'll say. You'll probably lose your pay
for ever more.' He was not angry and was only pulling my leg,
but I was cross with myself for having failed to do the job. Linda
was quite unharmed, but it was a very long time before I trusted
wind tyres again.

The wind tyres on the partridge shoot gave no such trouble
and the guns were in jovial mood after their lunch.

The birds had now to be driven into the wind but a straight
line of keepers can do this job, particularly since many of the
partridges were being driven back towards their own territory.
It is quite acceptable to drive birds twice in a day, but no more.
That would be sheer cruelty. The birds which now broke out
from the sides were probably the birds resident there and these
had to be ignored even if they went back over the beaters' heads.
Much could be done, however, with the birds which wanted to
get home. They travelled more slowly than they had in the
morning, now being tired and with the wind against them, and
they were easier targets for the guns. Keepers become anxious
when this happens because they can see a lot of their stock being
shot and not in the most difficult way, but it does make a difference to the bag.

There were usually four drives in the afternoon and at the end
of the day the bag was in the region of two hundred brace, not an
enormous number by pre-war standards.

At the end of the last drive, Mr Herbert thanked me for my
efforts, a gesture greatly appreciated since I had been working
all year for this day. That little recognition of the fact helped a
lot in the cold months ahead. The beaters were then dismissed,
those needing to be paid receiving their money immediately
from the head keeper. Then the bag was laid out for the

customary count, young birds being separated from the old. The squire and Mr Herbert then discussed the ratio of old to young before the birds were loaded back onto the cart and taken the short distance back to the game larder where they were hung again. The loaders went off to the gun-room to clean the guns and have a nip of whisky which always appeared from somewhere. Soon the housekeeper would appear with tea and rock buns, and the head keeper would make sure that each guest had a brace of birds put in his car. They had to be young birds because, although young partridges are delicious to eat, your teeth soon tell you if the bird is past its prime. On the market old birds only fetch half the price of younger ones.

As far as we were concerned, the day was over when the guns thanked the head keeper. They showed their appreciation by leaving a note in his hand as they shook it.

Mr Herbert put to one side all the gratuities he received during the season and, although he was not obliged to share this money, he always did so, for the Benacre beat-keepers worked hard all the year round. The share-out night was held in the week just before Christmas. All the beat-keepers gathered at the head keeper's lodge where beer had been laid on and then the money was divided, a useful bonus at that festive season, a sort of Aladdin's Christmas Club. Their weekly contribution had been the sweat of their brow and now they reaped the reward which they truly deserved. Their loyalty to Mr Herbert had been recognised, too.

8
Scents and Sensibility

There were times during my early years at Benacre when the keepers seemed to be waging war against some elements of the animal and human population. There is a lot of wisdom in the saying, 'Know thy enemy', and if we were going to pit our wits against the animals and poachers around us we had to know a great deal about them. I had already learned a lot from Friday and his generation who had acquired that knowledge from their predecessors. Man has, over the centuries, gathered an immense store of knowledge about the animals, and, fortunately, much of it has been retained and then passed on by successive generations of country people. As gamekeepers, we, too, were custodians of that heritage.

Most keepers have the greatest knowledge of the animals and birds they rear or tend, and those which are or could be enemies to them. Such predators are always referred to as vermin, the Latin derivation meaning 'worm' or 'parasitic worm', the implication being that they are parasites on the rest of the animal kingdom. I do not hold to this view since, as far as I am concerned, vermin are fleas and their kind. What most people refer to as vermin, I prefer to call the enemies of game. They have as much right to live in this world as has anything else. It is only because they interfere with the ways of man that attempts are made to keep them strictly under control.

Gamekeepers are not usually naturalists, at least not in the strictest sense of the word, but they do know a lot about nature, although few could tell you where or when they learned it. Not all of the knowledge is obviously useful. The hedgehog, for example, has spines which are really hairs modified to act as a protective jacket which few predators will breach, or even tackle. Some animals moult fairly quickly but not the hedgehog. Not all of its spines can be moulted at once or they would lose their value so they are shed and regrown singly over a period of time. When the hedgehog is threatened it coils itself into a ball, only its spines protruding, the spines moving and pointing in the direction of the threat. Contrary to popular belief, the hedgehog can move extremely quickly when it wants to and it is tragic that so many of them are crushed on the highway.

Foxes moult once a year, usually in early summer, their thick winter coat being replaced by a much shorter one which makes them look much slimmer. With the onset of autumn, more hairs grow to thicken the coat and as its density increases not all of the hairs can lie flat. They stand up and give the fox its robust appearance, but the thick coat belies its true size.

Some animals can change their coats very quickly as do the stoat and mountain hare. They are usually white in winter, a change possibly triggered by the sudden cold, and this camouflage is invaluable in the snow as well as helping with their body heat conservation.

Colour plays an important part in animal life, as camouflage and in warning systems. The rabbit is an excellent example of the latter; if startled, it thumps a foot on the ground and raises its white tail. Other rabbits, alerted by the thumping, see the white tail bobbing and are warned of danger. They, in turn, repeat the performance and then scamper away showing their white tails. Deer, especially the roe deer, also do this by fluffing out their light-coloured rump hairs which warns others.

Practically all animals have different kinds of teeth, but flesh-eating animals have very similar armour for seizing their prey. A fox has large canines between its incisors and molars and with this armament it can both seize and stab its prey, inflicting a serious or even fatal wound. This is also true of dogs, weasels and almost all animals which prey on others.

Another important aid is sight which can be used in various ways. Stoats and weasels, which stalk their prey, need to focus on their quarry, so their eyes face the front. Each eye has a field of vision which overlaps that of the other eye. This permits an accurate judgement of distances, but to look right or left the animal must move its head. When a stoat breaks cover, it looks straight ahead but then it turns its head to the right and to the left. This is very similar to the fox whose eyesight is not very sharp. The fox is quick to detect anything that moves but if you stand completely still he will run almost up to you before he realises that you are there. This failing has frequently led to his downfall. Other animals which live and feed in the open have all-round vision; these include deer, sheep, horses and rabbits and they need this facility to watch for danger even when they are feeding with their heads down. You will often see a horse, apparently engrossed in grazing, suddenly look up, completely alert for his all-round vision has detected some movement. He can also see a long way.

Friday always stressed that the most important thing to know about these animals was how they used and reacted to scent. Many creatures possess an acute sense of smell and it is pointless trying to stalk an animal if you are upwind of it for it will very quickly detect you. Animals use scent for all sorts of reasons; an otter leaves scent from its tail and is just one of many animals which mark out their territory by depositing such scents. They often scent their droppings with this liquid, which comes from glands under the tail. All animals seem to have territories to a greater or lesser degree and they are remarkably civilised in the way they respect one another's boundaries. As long as these are clearly marked, most animals stick to the unwritten and unspoken rule.

A rabbit has a large scent gland under its chin which it rubs against saplings, posts, stones and even the ground to mark its territory. Cats also use their chin or forehead to rub their scent onto objects, and even domestic dogs, reverting to the pack instinct, mark their territories. A dog which has been allowed out of the house after even a brief confinement will run around madly for a time, attend to the call of nature, and then scratch at the ground causing dirt to fly up. Dogs have scent glands between their toes and in performing this scratching they are clearly marking their territories.

Some deer have a similar device; fallow deer have a scent gland in the cleft of each hind foot and they leave a smell behind them. The fox has a very bushy tail, often referred to as its brush, and it can sometimes be seen waving its tail in all directions. Since there is a gland on the upper surface of the tail, it probably distributes its scent in this way. The squirrel's tail might also perform a similar role; it twitches its tail frequently, either when agitated or when displaying to a rival. When red deer stretch out their necks and pull back their lips they are able to sample the air to detect scents. This behaviour seems to be common in hooved animals; it is seen chiefly at breeding time and allows them to detect whether a potential mate is in season.

Snakes also use scent. The grass snake continually flicks out its tongue, allowing it to taste the air and the ground in front of it so that it can detect its prey and avoid danger.

The badger's scent gland, known as the musk gland, is under its tail. Since the badger is gregarious, it uses this gland to mark members of the group which allows quick recognition within its territory. Each group, therefore, must have a different scent to enable such differentiation to take place for an intruding badger is quickly detected. Badger-watchers have often seen a badger 'musking'; it lifts its tail and rubs its gland along the side of another member of the group. The smell to human nostrils is obnoxious. Both the stoat and the weasel can also produce an odious scent either to terrify an intended victim or to protect itself, rather as the American skunk does.

Hearing is another sense which is highly developed in many animals. Some, like dogs, snarl and grind their teeth as a warning to other animals and they combine this with a baring of the teeth as they adopt a crouching posture, ready to spring, the hair on their back usually standing up at the same time. This is almost always a bluff, but it does work. When a dog adopts this stance other dogs will usually slink away and few humans will attempt to pass a dog displaying such behaviour.

Cats have very acute hearing and will listen for their prey. I learned early in my career that it was impossible to approach a cat if I was wearing Wellington boots because they thumped against my legs and gave warning of my approach.

The pine marten has ears which face only forward and these it can focus in the same direction as its forward-facing eyes. In this case, the two senses are combined in the search for prey or the inspection of the scene ahead.

Foxes continually bark or howl at night to communicate with each other and have a dozen or more distinctive calls, each with its own meaning. These are best heard, and most frequently, in the winter during the breeding season. Similarly, the red deer stag in the rutting season can be heard bellowing at night and if you see him you will notice grass and pieces of turf hanging from his fearsome antlers. The bellowing is to intimidate rivals and to attract the attention of females and the stags which bellow loudest and longest acquire the largest share of the harem. Fallow bucks and sika stags behave in a similar way.

A good gamekeeper always takes the opportunity to study such animal behaviour and to make use of it whenever he can. He becomes at ease with it and most keepers are probably more at home among animals than they are with humans. Most people would feel very lonely and uncomfortable walking through woodland in the dead of night, but the keeper is at home there and far from alone. Even as a young keeper I spent many nights on watch in the Benacre woods and was always aware of hundreds of pairs of eyes watching me. I, an intruder on their patch, kept a look-out for intruders on what I considered to be mine. I have often wondered how far animals accept the gamekeeper. To some he is a provider and to others a protector. Perhaps King George VI summed up the work of the gamekeeper when he wrote, 'The wild life of today is not ours to dispose of as we please. We have it in trust. We must account for it to those who will come after.'

A good gamekeeper does have one companion on his nocturnal vigils — his night dog. The gamekeeper has more or less the same powers in law, on private land, as the policeman and the two wear uniforms, although not the same. If a gamekeeper sees people entering the land in daylight and he has reason to believe that they are in pursuit of game, he has the power to approach them and to find out who they are. If they tell him the truth and give their real names, which they can verify, he has the power to escort them from the land and to warn them that they will be reported. If, however, they refuse to give their names or give what the keeper suspects are false names, then he has the power to arrest. He would then hand them over to the police.

If the same situation occurs at night-time, the keeper has more powers. If he finds that the intruders are definitely in pursuit of game, he has the power of arrest and the power to confiscate all of their equipment, including guns, dogs, nets and anything else they are using to poach game. This is all very well in theory but for most of the time a keeper works alone, without back-up. If he suspects the presence of poachers on his beat he must investigate. One or two poachers are not difficult to deal with, but three or more can present problems. As with all such petty criminals, the larger the group, the braver and more brash they are. For this reason the night dog is an invaluable companion; the more aggressive the dog is, the less trouble the poachers give.

Gamekeeper's protection pistol, eighteenth century

Before the war the animals we used for this job were large, curly-coated retrievers or bull-terriers. A bull-mastiff would have been ideal, being large and formidable but, when over-excited, he was liable to attack the intruders and be difficult to restrain or retrieve by command or physical strength. Even the cost of his keep would have been too high. Today, alsatians perform the job extremely well but in the thirties they were not a common dog even though many had been brought back from mainland Europe after World War I. The curly-coated retriever fitted the bill perfectly being aggressive, large and capable of being trained and controlled. Selection of such a dog began with the litter. The pup required was the boldest, possibly the first to come forward. Other signs were a bold look in the eye and the way he looked at you. This pup was eventually taken away from the rest of the litter and kennelled on his own. The keeper then went to great trouble to ensure that he was the only person to feed and exercise the pup which was not allowed to become friendly with other people. He would keep the dog for about a year before attempting to train it, other than getting it to respond to its name. The young dog had plenty of exercise and more than the usual food ration with raw meat, bone and good biscuit so that it would grow a good, strong frame.

When the training started, the animal had to be completely obedient. It had to learn to walk to heel, to sit on command, to drop when ordered, to adopt the down or prone position and to stay there until told to do otherwise. This training would take the best part of a year and when we were training an animal the job had to be done to fit in with all of our other duties. When the dog was completely trained to obedience, the assistance of a colleague, preferably another trainer, was obtained to play the part of a poacher. It was important that whoever took on this role came nowhere near the dog except during the training sessions. The keeper, at this stage, had an idea but no definite knowledge of the level of the dog's courage. Some dogs are natural biters, but this is more of a nervous disorder and no indication of courage. A dog requires a great deal of courage to bite a man on command.

131

The second handler began a period of teasing the dog, initially in the dog's kennel. He would act in what the police describe as a suspicious manner. Dogs seem to know in a few seconds if someone is not behaving in a normal way. The man would arm himself with a whip-like stick and then slink past the kennel, flicking at the dog's face with the stick. The keeper was at hand and he encouraged the dog by saying, 'Watch him, watch him' or 'Get at him', which also excited the dog and gave him increasing confidence. This would continue for a few days or until the acting criminal had only to appear for the dog to become very excited merely by seeing him; he would growl and show his teeth and the hair would stand up along his back. Next the dog was taken on a strong short rope lead for a walk during which our 'criminal' would appear, usually from behind a hedge; if the groundwork had been properly done, the dog would immediately become suspicious and be on his guard. His ears would prick up and he would start to growl; the criminal would then approach with his stick and as he walked past he would flick the dog and then run. It was most important that the criminal appeared to be a coward. The dog had to win every time, which was something the 'criminal' had to understand. He had to test the dog to its limits but also know when to stop and when to retreat and run away into the distance. Naturally, the other keeper had to keep a firm hold of the dog's lead and had to constantly say 'Watch him, watch him'. The dog was trained to be confident and the handler would run with him in the direction of the disappearing criminal.

When the dog had become fully aggressive and would have bitten the criminal had he been able to reach him, the next step could be taken. Now the criminal armed himself with a thick padded sleeve, usually home-made; there was a leather handle on the inside onto which the criminal could hold to make sure that the sleeve did not come off. Wearing this sleeve the criminal would approach the dog and act aggressively. The dog would become very excited and want to get at him. The man would approach with his stick and stand just out of the dog's reach, holding the padded arm behind him. He would flick the dog's muzzle and legs with the stick which would sting but not hurt seriously. As he teased the dog, the handler would be encouraging it to 'Get at him' and to 'Attack, attack'. When the criminal thought the dog was sufficiently agitated, he would produce the sleeved arm and allow the dog to bite it. He had to be careful because a trained dog can bite viciously and his arm could have been bruised even through the padding. At the end of such a session, the criminal always ran away and, at the same time, threw the sleeve down. This would cause the dog to stop and bite at the sleeve, but this the handler quickly discouraged. When the criminal saw this happening, he would dance about and, if necessary, run back towards the dog. The dog would attempt to bite the man and not just his sleeve. The teasing and biting at the sleeve continued for quite a time and then the keeper brought in words of command. He would shout to the criminal, 'Stand still', and as soon as he did so he told the dog to leave both sleeve and man with the command, 'Leave'. The dog would be excited and want to continue but he would be pulled back. It was then that the obedience training came into its own. The dog had to learn to desist at once and to go down once the criminal was standing perfectly still. This was repeated over and over, while the dog was always kept on a short lead. Eventually, the dog was left in the down position while the keeper led the criminal away. When told to 'heel', the dog had to get up and go to his handler's side while he led the criminal away. Some dogs would want to bite the criminal while he was being led away, but this was discouraged and the dog would finally realise that his services were not required in that way.

There were other situations, though, where the dog was needed and for which he had to be properly trained. The keeper would leave him in the 'down' position while he himself walked towards the criminal. There the dog would stay until given a command to do otherwise. If the criminal then turned on him he would say firmly, 'To me' and 'Attack'. The dog had then to spring from his down position and go for the criminal who was on his guard with his sleeve ready. The short lead would still be attached to the dog and the trainer would pull this firmly to control the animal. Thereafter the exercises had simply to be repeated over and over so that the whole thing became routine. Next, the criminal had again to abandon the sleeve, and the practice of the dog attacking the man's arm was discontinued. This was quite logical because a dog with its teeth clamped onto an arm is vulnerable to an act like knifing by the criminal's free hand.

The progression from there in training the night dog was to introduce the box-muzzle, a heavily leathered device which completely encapsulated the dog's mouth and muzzle and was securely strapped to the animal's collar. Wearing this, the dog could not possibly bite, although he would try as hard as he could to remove it. He would then be allowed to attack the criminal; the man playing the part needed a lot of courage at this point. The keeper still had to insist on the dog's complete obedience at all times, particularly with the command 'Leave'. The criminal had, of course, to stand still and, having been told to leave, the dog was called first to heel and then down.

There would be some occasions when the keeper had to send his dog after a criminal who was escaping, possibly 200-300yd ahead. In a practice situation and in reality the dog would be told to 'Attack' and had to go straight in after the runner. He had then to bite and back off, going around the criminal barking all the time and harassing the man. This constant movement on the part of the dog ensured that it did not present an easy target for the poacher with gun, knife or club. When the keeper came on the scene he could tell the animal to leave, heel and go down, as long as the poacher was still. When that stage had been reached, the keeper could confidently take the dog out with him at night. Throughout the dog's life nobody but the keeper went near the animal, fed it or talked to it. Its only friend was the handler and it was exercised, as far as possible, at night. The keeper with a family tended not to have a night dog because a creature trained to this degree was likely to cause an accident.

Once the dog was fully trained, it would accompany the keeper on his night rounds. There were occasions when poachers would be found. If the keeper knew them he would

134

often call out their names for this disorientates the poacher who does not like to be recognised. The keeper would then call to the poachers to stand still; if they were abusive to him he would tell the dog to go down and to stay while he approached the criminals. They would have one eye on the dog whose ears would be up, its nose pointed straight at them. If they attempted to attack the keeper he would command the dog to come to him and to attack. It would go straight in. A good dog would bite a man between the legs and then leave, going on to the next poacher if there were several to be apprehended. This, as can readily be imagined, had a most demoralising effect on the poachers, as it would on any man, and caused extreme pain. They would soon ask for the dog to be called off which the keeper did before going forward to arrest the men. Very few poachers were prepared to face a trained dog or dogs, for some keepers had two dogs which they worked as a pair.

Dogs of this kind had to be trained frequently for any dog would rather be a friend than an enemy. About once a fortnight, particularly in the winter, the keeper would ask for his assistant to return to his role as the criminal and to tease the dog. Regular good feeding was essential, the dog received 1½lb of raw meat and bone every day along with the same weight of hard biscuits. This kept the dog in sound condition; as there was a lot of stress and excitement in its work, it exerted a great deal of energy which had to be replaced. Sadly, such dogs do not live long; they tend to age quickly especially if they are used regularly.

Night dogs are far more aggressive than the average police dog. The latter mingle frequently with the general public and such aggression would be intolerable. The gamekeeper's night dog was never used as an all-rounder for, once trained to distrust people, it was quite liable to bite at will without any encouragement. It was a liability which was the keeper's responsibility at all times. Should that keeper be ill for a period of time or have to go away, someone else had to look after the animal, a formidable task. It would take some time for that person to gain the dog's confidence to the point where he could take it for exercise. This could be achieved by not showing fear; at first, the dog's food was pushed under the door daily until gradually confidence was built between them and the dog would accept the new handler as a friend.

Another role often played by the night dog was that of search and find. Poachers in the woodland at night have an annoying habit of lying flat if they hear a gamekeeper approaching and they stay there until they think he has gone. The keeper alone cannot find them but the night dog was trained to 'wind' them. This meant that the keeper had to stay downwind of the mass of the wood so that the dog could pick up any scents. On scenting the presence of an intruder, the dog's ears would prick up and he became excited, warning the keeper that someone was there. To train the dog in this role, the keeper would walk him along the rides in the wood. The criminal, often called the stooge, would be hiding there and, as the dog approached, he would break cover and race towards the animal with his whippy stick. With this he would hit the dog and then run away, which infuriated the animal and made him want to reach the assailant. This was repeated for a length of time so that the dog was always on the alert in woodlands, constantly testing the wind with his nose, searching for the stooge.

The mistake of thinking that the night dog had a dreadful life was often made by people who did not understand the situation. He was not pampered like a household pet, but the keeper always looked after him very well and gave him much affection. He, being the only handler, received in return all the dog's affection and appreciation.

Once it became known that a gamekeeper had such a dog, it was not uncommon for poachers to leave his area completely alone. The training of such a dog was never undertaken lightly nor should anyone, even today, attempt such training unless well qualified to do so. Mistakes in a training programme have resulted in perfectly good dogs being turned into unapproachable monsters, but at Benacre the night dogs brought excellent results and were a credit to their trainers.

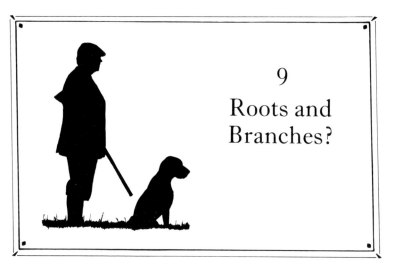

9
Roots and Branches?

There have been Foysters in East Suffolk for hundreds of years and I had always assumed them to be an old English family, but, in truth, the English connection is not very old. When I started to trace my family tree, the earliest Foyster I could find was in the year of the Spanish Armada, 1588. Her name is recorded as Christian Foyster and on 19 April that year she married one William Wright at Brundish. This Foyster must have had close relatives because, although she changed her name on marriage, the Foyster name was quite common in Suffolk for a long time afterwards and still lives on there today. The first Foyster, or Foysters, came from the Netherlands and their Dutch name was Devuyster. Holland was then a Spanish possession where Protestants were persecuted. The Devuysters may have come to England to escape persecution or because they possessed a skill much in demand at the time.

The Foysters eventually came to Benacre and in 1829 a John Foyster married Maria Raven there. Then, in 1864, another John Foyster, possibly his son, married Mary Flat, also in Benacre. There were two other Foyster marriages in Benacre at about that time; in 1862, Ellen Foyster married James Cutter, and, in 1864, Elizabeth married Alfred Folkard. The two Johns were certainly my ancestors and Ellen and Elizabeth were probably great great aunts.

The cafe in Wrentham, 1938

Benacre is a very small place as is nearby Covehithe. When I was a young keeper, everybody knew everyone else in the villages and for miles around. My mother's family and ancestors, the Tinks, were also of Dutch origin and they lived in Wrentham, South Cove and Covehithe. Their name was originally Tencke. Since all of these tiny villages and hamlets have so few occupants I must be related in some way to practically every family which has been in the area for any length of time, although to some connections, should they exist, I would perhaps rather not admit.

On the edge of Covehithe lived an old lady called Liza. A big woman by any standards, she swore like a fishwife with a vocabulary which would have been a trooper's envy. We often saw her with sleeves rolled up to reveal arms the thickness of an ordinary man's leg. On the odd occasions when, as a small boy, I went to church with my mother, I always seemed to sit behind her. She always wore a black hat and coat but suffered terribly from dandruff, which affliction was highlighted by the colour of her clothes. I certainly paid more attention to that than I did to the sermon. Gradually, Liza became mentally unstable. She had never been a pleasant person, particularly to children, and

138

seemed to think that small boys were the lowest form of life. Liza lived by herself and had for company only a very large labrador type of dog, the size of a great dane. It was completely mad and not even the bravest postman would go through the garden gate if it was loose. The day eventually arrived when Liza was so unstable that it was necessary to remove her from the cottage to an institution. A motor ambulance had arrived, complete with two men in white coats, and the local constable was also in attendance. They had difficulty in gaining access to the house; Liza was cursing and threatening them from her bedroom window, while in the garden, the dog, frothing at the mouth and baring its teeth, was trying to jump over the gate. I was, at the time, in the keeper's cottage not far away and the constable came for me to put the dog down. I collected my gun, cycled to Liza's cottage and shot the animal.

I have fonder memories of a thatched cottage named Warren House, home of a man called Beaver Eade who had been in the carpet trade. He was retired and his daughter kept house for him. My youngest sister, Dorothy, had once been a maid at Warren House and on Sunday evenings my father, mother and I were invited there for tea. Miss Eade had a beautiful gramophone with a large and ornate horn which sounded much better than the smaller portables which were then in vogue. On it she played classical music and my mother loved to hear her record of the Academy of St Martin-in-the Fields playing 'Ave Maria'. My love of music stems from those Sunday evenings at Warren House. For tea we always had very thin bread and butter and, in the summer, cucumber sandwiches. Old Beaver, with his long beard, was a bit of an old rascal, not averse to telling the occasional naughty joke, much to Miss Eade's annoyance. She had been trained in Red Cross work and was very good to my family. Once I slid down a straw stack and, as my feet hit the ground, my head went forward and my teeth sank into my knee. Mother applied ointment and bandages to the wound but it festered and refused to heal. Miss Eade noticed this and came to our house on her bicycle where she dressed the knee and applied peroxide to it. It used to hurt like the devil but the treatment healed the wound quickly. We did not normally take much notice of such cuts but Miss Eade, a spinster and rather bossy, insisted on dressing mine.

Beaver Eade had an ancient twelve-bore shotgun with which he delighted in shooting rabbits from his bedroom window, much to his daughter's distress. Since the house was near an extensive rabbit warren, he had plenty of targets. Unlucky, too, was the cock pheasant which strayed within his range for it would be peppered with shot. Old Billy, the keeper, would have been furious had he known but he never found out. Beaver Eade was quite a character and a hardy gentleman who would boast how, on winter mornings, he woke to find ice on his whiskers.

The local parson was called Wingfield and he lived in the vicarage at Benacre, a beautiful house, with his wife who showed kindness to everyone. He had the livings of both Benacre and Covehithe. After the service, he always insisted on giving us a lift home in his car, although I would have preferred to walk. My mother was well thought of in church circles, a good worker and a leading member of the Mothers' Union.

The church organist was Mrs Braben, and I cannot help feeling that she was not very good at it. The glory of an organ is the chords played on it but unfortunately Mrs Braben played with only two fingers. One day we heard that she wanted to join our team of bell-ringers, but the request was not greeted with great enthusiasm. We pursued another activity in the belfry as well as ringing bells and thought that, as the only lady, she might not approve of it. A crate of brown ale was produced every practice night for bell-ringing was a thirsty business, and we suspected that Mrs Braben might try to stop our liquid consumption. I was not a particularly good ringer, but my father was and the whole team had developed the smuggling in of the beer crate to a fine art. What was more, and the reason we felt that our light refreshment was sanctioned by a higher authority, was that the beer was provided by Richard Gooch, Sir Robert's younger brother and an active member of our team. He loved a bit of fun and also had a passion for fast cars. He always referred to our family as 'Forster' and when he offered us a lift home in one of his cars he would ask my father if he was afraid to ride with him. Father always gave the same reply that if Mr Richard was not afraid to drive, then he had no qualms about travelling with him. We must have been an odd sight stumbling into the smart Lagonda after a few bottles of ale.

For several weeks Mrs Braben was given tenuous excuses; the ladder to the belfry was unsafe for a lady and was being stabilised; the bell-rope she was to use was being replaced; there were some unsafe floor-boards and we were having difficulty repairing them. One evening, however, just as we were about to begin, we heard her calling up from the foot of the ladder. We did consider pretending that we had not heard her but her high, penetrating voice would have obviated this lie. My father was sent down to lend assistance to her ascent and, after much pulling and pushing, her round face appeared above the trap-door. Reluctant hands pulled her into the belfry as we feigned pleasure at seeing her and, at the same time, covered the beer crate with our coats. Mr Richard, our natural leader, decided that, since Mrs Braben was there, we should demonstrate the art of bell-ringing. She was taught how to pull up the bell and was assigned to one of the smaller ones for practice. It had been made very clear to the novice that a belfry could be a dangerous place once the bells started to ring and their ropes went up and down. When the bells swing and the rope comes down it forms a half loop in front of the ringer. Mrs Braben positioned herself badly and, when the rope went back up, it circled her and took her up with it. She was known to the village children as Mrs Lump because of her dumpy shape and her nickname came to my mind as I watched her being drawn upwards like a sack of corn in a mill. We were all at our own ropes and were initially powerless to help her. It looked as if she would crack her head on the ceiling; we all, I am sure, held our breath, but she stopped just short of it and Mr Richard hurried over to disentangle her. She was quite shaken by the experience and very pale as he offered further assistance by driving her home. We were never again joined in our belfry by Mrs Braben although every time we saw her we particularly asked when we should see her up there again. The story quickly went round our community and it was difficult not to laugh out loud when she waddled into church the following Sunday. I can still picture her now, indelicately suspended in time and motion by that rope. We certainly relished our beer after she left the belfry on that memorable evening.

Our church was a small building which stood on the ruins of what must have once been a large abbey, dissolved during the reign of Henry VIII. There was also, nearby, a large settlement called North Hales, but this fell into the sea long before my time. Its ruins must now lie about 7 or 8 miles out to sea.

Opposite the church there was a fairly large building which had once been a pub. Since it had reverted to being a private dwelling called Anchor House, the pub was probably called The Anchor. It was closed down by one of the squires, it was said, on the grounds that when he came out of church his sensibilities were offended by the sight of the locals swilling

The binder at work in the field

down beer. The simple solution, since he owned the pub, was to close it. When I knew the house, it was occupied by Mr Braben, Mrs Lump's father-in-law. He was a tall, serious old man and an extremely good gardener. With him lived his unmarried son, Ted, who worked for his uncle as part of the threshing team. This uncle owned a traction engine and threshing tackle and with it they travelled from farm to farm and hired themselves out whenever a corn stack had to be threshed. In those days the sheaves of corn were taken by cart from the fields and made into a stack, complete with gable ends, and then it was thatched to keep out the weather. The tenants of Church Farm and Field Farm would sell the grain to raise extra money for Christmas. My father worked with the horses at Field Farm and on one memorable occasion the wheels of the traction engine sank into the ground as it rumbled into the farmyard. It was completely stuck and Mr Braben was convinced that his precious machine would be there forever. My father offered to pull out the machine, although Mr Braben was very doubtful that such a feat could be accomplished. My father said nothing but left the man in his dejected state and went away round a corner. Five minutes later he returned leading six horses. Mr Braben laughed when he saw this, convinced that they would not even budge the engine. My father quietly attached to it the horses in their traces and went to the head of the team. Those six Suffolk Punches drew the traction engine from the mud at their first attempt without difficulty.

Ted Braben's sister, Daisy, lived near us. She had married a fisherman called Oliver Bird, a trawler-man, and whenever he came home he would bring my mother the most wonderful prime fish. He was allowed to bring a certain amount home with him but he never ate it himself having seen enough of it at sea.

Electricity did not come to the village until after the war, and the radio to which I listened so keenly was powered by batteries. It was also rented because a wireless was an expensive item and people used to rent them after the war had ended. The coming of electricity was a wonderful thing; at first we had one light and, in the kitchen, one plug which was a great asset since it meant that we could have an electric kettle. This would boil in five minutes instead of the previous thirty taken by the kettle on the hob.

Before the days of electricity, our light came from rather elegant paraffin lamps which gave a good light but also a lot of heat. The cleaning of the inner glass and trimming of the wicks was a daily routine always undertaken by mother. The paraffin for the lamps was delivered by a man on a bicycle behind which was a trailer for the containers. There were other doorstep deliveries from the butcher, the baker and the milkman. The latter also rode a bicycle with churns attached to the handlebars and from these churns he ladled the milk into the housewife's container. We had no milk-bottles; they were yet to be seen in Covehithe. To earn a living, the milkman had to rise very early to milk his cows, having first brought them in from the field, and he had to deliver early for nobody wanted milk at lunchtime.

Groceries were also delivered, but one of us had to take the order to the shop at Wrentham beforehand. My mother wrote down all her requirements in a book which was taken to the grocer's. When the boy delivered the provisions, he brought back the book so that mother could check that everything was there. She then paid him and he cycled away on his heavy old bicycle.

At school I enjoyed taking in the grocery book for I was allowed to buy some toffee, my favourite sweet. The grocer broke it from a slab into smaller pieces; when bought it was rock hard, but it gradually softened in my pocket and I would eat it in class. I always let it melt in my mouth and never chewed it for the teacher would have spotted that, although I was caught on a couple of occasions.

Near Warren House was a row of cottages in one of which lived a family called Snelling. The father worked at Porter's Farm and his oldest son was a deaf mute who was very intelligent. This lad was very quick at writing which was his prime method of communication. He had a brother called Reg, known as Bum, but how he acquired this nickname I do not know. Occasionally, he would come out with Jack and me but owing to

144

a speech impediment never attracted the girls. He was always the odd one out but he still liked to come along with us. His failure with girls never seemed to bother him but when Jack and I 'clicked' with some girls, it was always Reg who went home alone. Perhaps I always managed to find the good side of people but there was hardly anybody in the area I did not like in some way. There were times when we did not want Reg with us but we never had the heart to send him away.

Percy Folkard was another character I remember from those days. He looked rather Japanese and wore what seemed to be enormous boots. He was short and thick-set with very broad shoulders. His wife, an old fuss-pot, was my godmother and a great friend of my mother. She had no children of her own and always called me Jackie.

These, then, were the people among whom I grew up. How much each of them influenced me and how I cannot say, but, to a greater or lesser extent, they must all have played a part. If nothing else, they provided me with fond memories which I still cherish.

Do I still, I wonder, use a spade as I was taught by Mr Spall? Do I still load a gun as Friday showed me? There is probably at least one young keeper who cleans his gun exactly as I do and as Friday did before me. What Friday and the others taught me about the countryside and its creatures I have passed on to others.

A gamekeeper had to be flexible for not only was he expected to work irregular hours, but also to wear many hats in the course of a year. One moment he was talking to beaters and other keepers and the next to members of the nobility and even royalty. This was especially true when he had to act as a loader on shooting days.

Every keeper had to be skilled in the art of loading and well practised in the use of shotguns. Usually, and certainly at Benacre, loaders were trained to do the job properly and before I was allowed to load for a gentleman, Friday taught me the correct method and then made sure that I knew exactly how to do so in practice. He instilled into me that I was handling two guns at the same time; one loaded gun in the wrong hands is highly dangerous, he used to say, but two are a disaster.

The act of handing a loaded shotgun to the shooter had to be a well-practised drill. There were several occasions when I acted as a loader for one of the guests at the hall on a partridge-shooting day. Naturally, I had to turn up in my best keeper's suit made of Irish twill. I was always introduced to the man for whom I would be loading and then directed towards the guns and cartridges. As the weapons were worth, by today's values, anything from £10,000 to £15,000, care had to be taken not to dent them, scratch them or allow them to be damaged in any way. The guns would be removed from their cases and the oil in which they had been put away cleaned off. A cartridge fired down an oily barrel could have had disastrous results so the barrels were dried off with a rod or a pull-through and the guns transferred from their case to a leather or canvas slip. This had a strap and I preferred to carry the guns in their slips with the barrel pointing downwards, purely for my own comfort.

Guests usually bought their cartridges in bulk and the loader would fill his cartridge bag from the box and put the remaining ammunition onto the carriage which was used to transport the guns. In this way it was easily accessible when the cartridge bag needed replenishing, although the average bag would hold two or three hundred and be quite heavy. Sometimes the loader would carry the guest's raincoat and, if he were not using it, his shooting stick, too. He was thus well encumbered but the loaders did at least have the privilege of travelling with the guns in their carriage.

On arriving at the first stand, the guns would be kept in their slips until the last moment. When the head keeper blew his whistle to signal the start of the first drive, the two guns would be loaded and one of them handed to the shooter with the safety catch on. As the partridges began to come over, the shooter would loose one shot at a bird and then hand the weapon back to the loader with just one cartridge used, and the safety catch on. The loader always took the discharged gun in his left hand and handed over the loaded one with his right. On all such changeovers the gun barrel had to point directly upwards. The barrel only pointed down when the gun was being loaded and it always had to be pointed away from the shooter while this was being done. As soon as the gun was ready, the loader would turn to watch the birds flying towards the shooting party. The guests were not always as alert as they should have been and it was quite in order, if the loader saw a bird which had not been spotted, for him to say discreetly to the guest, 'Partridge ahead, 2 o'clock.' This was sufficient to draw his attention to the approaching bird.

Some of the guns were not experienced shots and would not mind asking a loader's advice as to how, for example, he should tackle two oncoming birds. The loader had to have the experience to help in such a case.

I always watched carefully the arcs and angles described by the gun as it was being aimed at a bird. The shooters were spaced 40yds apart and it was all too easy for a man to become engrossed in the bird he was after; he could swing with the bird, oblivious of the fact that he was going along the line and might have shot someone. When I saw this happening I would quickly say, 'Careful sir. You're too far round.' It was my job to do that. If the shooter himself realised what was happening, his course was to stop, put up his gun, do a complete turn-about and take the partridge from the rear. The pickers-up were always far enough away for this to be a safe ploy.

There have been occasions when I have been saddled, unwittingly, with the sort of shooter who is a liability to himself and to others, the man who has claimed beforehand that he knows it all and turns up to the shoot immaculately dressed and sporting a pair of perfectly matched guns; in reality he is a novice. One memorable day I was acting as loader to such a gun, and by the end of the shoot I was exhausted. His greatest fault was swinging his gun along the line, as I have just mentioned, but he swung to both right and left. He also needed watching when other guns knew the drill. There comes a time on every drive when the beaters are about to come within range of the line of guns. Mr Herbert would then blow a long blast on his whistle,

147

Gentleman with valet-loader demonstrating the correct, safe method of handling and reloading two guns. The loader takes the discharged gun in his left hand and hands over the loaded one with the right. The gun barrel points directly upwards and is only pointed downwards when the gun is being loaded

the guns having been warned at the start of the day not to shoot anything in front once the whistle had been blown. They could shoot to their rear but had in no way to endanger the lives of the beaters at their front. My man had me constantly on tenter-hooks as I was sure he would swing his gun to the front at any moment.

Fortunately, I was able to constrain my shooter that day and he did no damage to himself nor to anyone around him, but I heaved a sigh of relief when the day was over. Mr Herbert, who had realised my dilemma early in the day, suggested to the host that perhaps it would be prudent not to invite that gun again until he had gained more experience elsewhere and at the expense of someone else's nerves.

On one shoot a beater was struck in the face by a pellet and it happened because a gun fired to the front after the whistle had gone. The beater was not badly hurt and it was impossible to say which gun was to blame, but the day was soured by the inci-

148

dent. Regrettably, such things happened from time to time, as they still do.

I have been hit by shotgun pellets and, although it did not hurt badly at the time, they sting severely afterwards. They do not penetrate far but they are very hot.

When the head keeper had signalled the end of the drive, the guns were taken by the loader who made sure that they were unloaded, for a loaded gun in a slip case can be lethal. The guns were then replaced in the slips until the next drive.

Some guns were quite amenable to a disjointed running conversation with their loader throughout the day but others preferred not to talk at all, except when really necessary. It was never, in either case, up to the loader to initiate conversation; a chatterbox does not make a good loader for, frequently, the guns were business people who were in the countryside to escape from the daily noise which usually surrounded them. Some were there for private thought as well as for the shooting and did not react kindly if they were disturbed too often. Conversely, however, Herbert Thrower would become very agitated by noise from the line — banter from the guns, not the beaters.

149

Occasionally, the gun would pull out his hip-flask which he might pass to his loader. It was quite in order to thank him and to take a drink which was very welcome on a cold day as most shooting days were.

Most of the shooters were absolute gentlemen but some could be grumpy or nervous. The loader had to be able to adapt himself to cope with all types. Birds have acute hearing and if they hear noise from the line they veer away. Nervous guns would want to shout at their neighbour but this had to be discreetly and tactfully discouraged.

One of the loader's unwritten duties was to help the pickers-up by noting how many birds his shooter had downed. Some guns were prone to exaggerate when telling the pickers-up where their birds had fallen and how many there were. The wise picker-up always looked to the loader to have these kills and their direction substantiated.

Some of the guns who came to Benacre on a fairly regular basis would ask for a particular loader, and it was always gratifying to be asked for in this way. It gave the gun confidence to know that he could trust implicitly the man who was standing behind him with a loaded gun.

There were times when serving army officers came to a shooting day and they often brought their own loaders, either their batman or, perhaps, even their own gamekeeper. Such visiting loaders would go across at the start of the day and introduce themselves to the head keeper, explain for whom they were loading and ask if there were any special instructions. Etiquette in such matters was very important.

At the end of the day it was the loader's responsibility to make sure that the guns were cleaned, oiled and properly put away. Today, we see American shooters with their pump-action guns while others favour over-and-unders, but before the war side-by-sides were the only proper guns used on a shoot. The weapons were taken into the gun-room of Benacre Hall, dismantled, and the barrels thoroughly cleaned with a rod. If there had been a lot of shooting that day, a phosphor-bronze brush was put through the barrels to take away any leading which

Double-barrel, muzzle-loading shotgun, in use prior to 1860

Shot and powder flasks for use with muzzle-loading gun

might have accumulated from the shot, for when used intensively over a short period the shotguns became quite hot. The caps used in cartridges then were not like the ones used today and, if the guns were not cleaned immediately after shooting, the barrels would be red rusty and almost ruined. After the phosphor-bronze brush had been used, the barrels were thoroughly oiled and cleaned out with a mop or tow. When they were perfectly clean, the barrels were slightly oiled. The complete weapon was then lightly oiled all over and returned to its case. Before being used again, this oil had to be removed completely, but only on the morning of the shoot.

Before the invention of the breech-loading shotgun in the mid-nineteenth century, most shooting was done with muzzle-loaders so the practice of driving game over the guns was not employed. Partridges were 'walked up' and shot over pointers; the guns would walk in line, their loaders carrying these enormous weapons. Some guns went into the field with three such weapons and two loaders. The pointers used to range ahead of the line of men and when they came upon a covey of partridges these dogs would live up to their name. The handler would then shout to the dog, 'To-ho', and it would point. It adopted a stance and stood like a statue, nose pointing straight forward, the body rigid, one foot raised and its tail out straight. While the dog was 'on the point', partridges rarely moved, and this allowed the guns to walk into range. It was the handler's skill to know when the dog had found a covey and the dog's to hold down those birds. Once the line was within range, the loader quickly handed a gun to the shooter, the covey was sprung by the pointer on a command from the handler, and the birds went off in all directions, at which point the shooters fired.

For pheasant shoots, similar tactics were employed by dogs like spaniels who were used because the pheasant, unlike the partridge, squats until the last moment. Loading in those days must have been a tiring task for the old muzzle-loaders were heavy guns in any case but, carried all day, must have become an increasing burden.

Gamekeepers at Benacre did not keep their guns in hard cases

152

Thomas Horsley (Coney Street, York) Patent no 374 drop-down-barrel, breech-loading action shotgun, 1862

as did most of the shooters who visited the estate. When the gun was not in use, it was wrapped in a long puttee, probably left over from World War I. The gun, in its puttee, was then slipped into a canvas sling, protected from all the knocks and scratches it would otherwise have suffered as it travelled with the keeper, strapped to the crossbar of his bicycle. Our guns were of a good age and their metal was bright; they had, therefore, to be well cleaned and oiled after every use because even fingerprints would leave rust marks on them.

Our guns may have been old, but there were older pieces at Benacre. One of these was an old double-barrel hammer gun made by Thomas Horsley of York. It was one of the earliest breech-loading shotguns made, under British Patent 374, and Friday told me that it had been made in 1862. It was a fine old gun, made with Damascus barrels, a white metal. The cylinders were made from strips of metal sweated together to form a true cylinder. Such guns were fine when used with black powder but not for the ammunition we were using then which would have burst the barrels.

Westley Richards (Bond Street, London) breech-loading, pin-fired, double-barrel shotgun showing pin cartridges

A regular shooter at Benacre was our local vicar, Mr Wingfield, for whom I frequently acted as loader. I had as much faith in the man as he had in the Almighty, but one day that faith was shattered. It was a dreadfully wet day and everyone on the field was wearing a raincoat, myself included. I was very proud of my coat since it was very expensive and I had saved up for it for months. It was a rubberised riding mackintosh and this was its first outing. Mr Wingfield, although perfectly dressed in his tweed suit, still sported his clerical collar. I was highly amused at the paradox as I pictured him singing 'All things bright and beautiful' and then saw him blasting God's little creatures. On this particular day, the drive had finished and I had gone forward to pick up a couple of birds. As the rain had eased off and the sun come out, I began to feel warm so I removed my precious raincoat and hung it over a stick. Suddenly behind me there was a loud bang. To this day I do not know precisely what happened but the vicar had somehow managed to shoot my new coat. There it hung, riddled with shot and completely ruined. I did not shed tears, although I was close to doing so. Nor was I angry. The sensation was more one of numbness on my part, and the vicar was in a state of shock. He looked at the coat in horror and then came over to me. He could not apologise enough and offered to buy me a new coat, an offer which I readily accepted since mine was beyond repair. The new coat took weeks to come but when it did arrive I made a point of wearing it to church. The hymn after the sermon was 'Holy, Holy, Holy'. It was pure coincidence, but whenever I hear that hymn now I think of my poor old holey mackintosh.

10
Fesauntes
and Patryches

Friday taught me all he knew about the partridge and pheasant, but I wanted to know something of their history and for this he referred me to books. One afternoon, therefore, I went to Southwold library and there began my research into the two birds I spent much of my time nurturing. The common partridge is indigenous to these islands. How or when it arrived is not known. The French or red-legged partridge is an import. As its name suggests, it came here from France, but much incorrect information has been published, even in recent years, about its introduction. The bird is found in all south-west European countries. The credit for the detection of the true story of its introduction into England belongs to Lord Leicester. In 1921 he sent to the *Field* magazine a copy of a letter which had been found in the National Library in Paris. It had been sent from London and was dated 9 October 1673. It was from Charles Colbert, Marquis de Croisy, the ambassador of Louis XIV of France, to Charles II, King of England, and was addressed to Jacques de Saumary, Comte de la Corre, Grand Master of Waters and Forests and Captain of the Castle of Chambord. The letter asked him to supply Favennes de Mouchant, the king of England's gamekeeper, with *'perdrix rouges'*. These 'red partridges' were to be released in the parks of Richmond and Windsor. If the request was met with immediately, the first

French partridges must have arrived here in the late autumn of 1673. This is, of course, only surmise, for whether the birds were delivered we do not know.

The famous diarist Samuel Pepys heard in 1666 of a visit by Sir Robert Long to the royal court in France when, in a single day, the king of France and his fellows shot more than three hundred partridges.

By the end of the eighteenth century, French partridges were well established in many parts of England. The seventeenth-century introduction seems to have been less than successful, for no more was heard of the Frenchman. In 1779, however, just over a hundred years later, the Marquess of Hertford established the bird on his estate in Suffolk. There had been other attempts elsewhere but all had failed.

The common pheasant was established in England much earlier. It was probably introduced by Roman settlers who came here in the wake of the legions. Wealthy Romans certainly enjoyed eating pheasant.

There is a record of magpies, partridges and a pheasant being served at a meal at Waltham in 1059, but some authorities doubt the validity of this reference which dates from 1177.

The abbot of Malmesbury obtained in, or soon after, 1100, a licence to kill hares and pheasants. By 1299, a pheasant cost 4d at a time when you could buy a pair of woodcock for 1½d, a mallard for the same price and a plover for 1d.

St Thomas à Becket ate a pheasant the day he died in 1170. One of his monks remarked that the martyr 'dined more heartily and cheerfully that day than usual'.

Leland, the historian, records that, at the enthronement of George Neville as Archbishop of York during the reign of Edward IV, part of the banquet consisted of two hundred 'fesauntes'.

There is an entry in the Privy Purse Expenses of Elizabeth of York for November which tells of a payment of 5s to 'Richard Mylner of Byndfeld for bringing a present of fesauntes cokkes to the Queen to Westminster'.

In 1512 the Household Book of Henry Percy, 5th Earl of

Woodcock and family

Northumberland, was begun, in which there are several references to pheasants. He lived at Alnwick, among other places, where the pheasant seems to have been in short supply if the price is any indication. While pheasants cost 1s each, many other birds were much cheaper. Also costing 1s were herons, bitterns, curlews and peacocks, while spoonbills were 7d, geese were 3d, or 4d at the most, and for just 2d the earl could buy a partridge or a mallard. Even cheaper were chickens, plovers, woodcocks, redshanks and other ducks, but more expensive than all others priced was the crane at 1s 4d. He also bought swans for his table but we do not know what he paid for these.

In 1522, there was published a *History of England*. It was written by Polydore Vergil, an Italian who had been sent to England many years earlier by Pope Alexander VI. In his history, he explains that 'the cheefe food of the Englishmen consisteth in flesh. They have an infinite number of birdes, as well

158

fostered in the howse as breeding in their woodds. Of wilde burdes these are most delicate, partiches, pheasaunts, quayles, owsels, thrusshes and larckes.'

In 1536, Henry VIII found it necessary to issue a proclamation as a measure to preserve the partridges, pheasants and herons over an area stretching from the Palace of Westminster to St Giles-in-the-Fields and from there to Islington, Hampstead, Highgate and Hornsey Park. Anyone who killed or in any way harmed the birds there was to be imprisoned. The king certainly rewarded the men who bred them for in the Privy Purse Expenses of King Henry VIII there are several references to such recompense. Two entries are dated 16 November 1532. The first records, 'Item — the same day paied to the fesaunt breder in rewarde — nine shillings and four pence'. The second is a payment of two crowns nine shillings and four pence to 'the preste [priest] the fesaunt breder at Eltham' on the twenty-fifth day. In December comes the entry, 'the 22nd daye paied to the french Preste the fesaunte breder for to bye him a gowne and other necesarys — fifteen shillings'.

How these pheasants were caught is rather uncertain but in the Household and Privy Purse Accounts of the L'Estranges of Hunstanton we find, 'Item, a Fesant kylled with the Goshawke' and 'two Fesants and two Partridges killed with the hawks'.

How the birds were caught is not always recorded; they are usually referred to simply as having been 'brought in', but the bringer seems always to have been rewarded. Here, in modern English, are four examples found in the Household and Privy Purse Accounts of the Princess Mary:

January 1537 — Item, given to Hunte, yeoman of the poultry, for bringing to her grace two live pheasants . . . 7 shillings 6 pence.
April 1537 — Item, given to Grene the partridge taker for bringing a couple of pheasants to my lady's grace . . . 3 shillings 9 pence.
January 1538 — Item, given to my lady Carow's servant for bringing a live pheasant . . . 2 shillings.
January 1544 — Item, given to Hawkyn, servant of Hertford, for bringing a pheasant and partridges . . . 3 shillings 4 pence.

The price of birds, or possibly the generosity of the donor, obviously fluctuated. The 'value' of pheasants also altered through the centuries and a good indicator of this is the punishment imposed for taking them illegally.

In 1520, a statute was passed forbidding anyone to catch without licence pheasants and partridges with 'engines' (traps), on penalty of a fine of £10, an enormous sum in those days. By the reign of Elizabeth I, the taking of pheasants and partridges by night was punished by a fine of 20s for a pheasant and 10s for a partridge. Those who could not pay were imprisoned for one month and then bound over not to repeat the offence. James I imposed even stricter penalties: 'No person shall kill or take any pheasant or partridge in pain of twenty shillings or imprisonment for every fowl or egg, and to find sureties in £20 not to offend in the like kind.' Nor was any person permitted 'to buy or sell any pheasant or partridge upon pain or forfeit of twenty shillings for every pheasant and ten shillings for every partridge'. The illicit taking of birds must have increased because just a few years later it is recorded that 'Every person having hawked at or destroyed any pheasant or partridge between the first of July and the last of August forfeited forty shillings for every time so hawking, and twenty shillings for every pheasant or partridge so destroyed or taken'.

Some people were allowed to take the birds but only at certain times of year. Lords of the manor and their servants could take pheasants and partridges in their own grounds and precincts in the daytime between Michaelmas, 29 September, and Christmas. Nobody else had any right to take the birds.

An entry in the household expense of Sir John Howard, afterwards Duke of Norfolk, for April 1467 records at Ipswich 'Item — twelve fesawnts pryse twelve shillings'. If there were pheasants at Ipswich there might well have been some at Covehithe or Wrentham a few miles away.

There have been several changes in the English pheasant population since the first birds were introduced. These were called the Old English blackneck although they have almost ceased to exist as a pure type. In about 1750 the Chinese or ring-

160

neck variety was introduced into England, followed in 1840 by the Japanese pheasant. The last to come with any success was the Mongolian. With all the interbreeding which has followed these foreign introductions, it is now virtually impossible to find a pure-bred bird in the wild. There is also now another type called a melanistic mutant which looks like the Japanese but is really the result of cross-breeding.

Pheasants on the rearing-field are first mentioned in a poem published in 1790 by Henry James Pye. Where in England this was going on, he does not say, nor do we really know if it was common practice at the time.

In 1800, Peter Hawker wrote, about pheasants:

> They are frequently kept in aviaries, and often intermixt with pheasants of another country, which produces a very fine breed. I have frequently kept young ones, for some time, by hatching the eggs under a hen, which they follow, whilst young; but no sooner are they capable of a short flight, than they betake themselves to the woods and common fields.

In 1814, Colonel George Hanger produced a book in which he gave instructions for the care and feeding of young pheasants in the coop, a volume followed a few years later by *The Art of Preserving Game* in which Lawrence Rawstorne explained methods of rearing pheasants.

There is a creamy-coloured pheasant known as the Bohemian. Another type is the melanistic mutant, which first appeared in about 1927. It takes its name from the Greek word meaning 'black', referring to its pigmentation. A true melanistic never has the ring marking on its neck. In some parts of Suffolk there was also a pheasant called the Breckland; it was smaller than other pheasants. It did not appear in East Suffolk but it was very common around Cambridge and Thetford.

'Sportsmanlike' is a term whose definition has altered over the last three hundred years. Originally, pheasants, partridges and smaller birds were shot by men using flintlocks and powder flasks. Partridge-driving was first introduced at Heveringham, Lord Huntingfield's property in Suffolk, in 1845. One of the earliest references to shooting game 'on the wing' is of George I shooting flying partridges in Windsor Great Park, but few, it would appear, had much success with moving birds. However, shooting at sitting birds was considered to be perfectly sportsmanlike into the early years of the nineteenth century. To our minds, the partridge-shooting of those days would have been a tedious business, the guns being out sometimes all day with their heavy and cumbersome equipment and dogs for a bag which scarcely justified the effort.

That day in the library, the knowledge I gained about the history of keepering somehow added to the pride I was learning to take in my job. It was at almost the same time that I realised that, done properly, gamekeeping was not a job but a way of living.

I had grown up in Covehithe and Wrentham without ever being told very much about the places I knew and took for granted. There were no references to local history at school and it was not until after school that I began to absorb information about the area. I went to bell-ringing for many months before one of the men told me that the five bells of Covehithe church were among the oldest in England and the best toned. Nor had I, until then, realised where the Five Bells pub had got its name. I knew the church had five bells but I had never connected the two pieces of information.

Covehithe church itself had a long and rather complicated history. The small church, with its huge tower, completely out of proportion, stands among the ruins of an earlier building, of which the tower was a part. The original large church was probably built in the fifteenth century by a wealthy vicar, William Yarmouth, financially assisted by some of his friends. Why they wanted such a structure is hard to tell for there can never have been enough parishioners to fill it. Even when North Hales still existed there were only about three hundred people in the parish. The church was obviously wealthy and contained many treasures. During the dissolution of the monasteries, the Parliamentary Commissioner, Dowsing, sacked the building

162

Covehithe church today — little changed since my time

and his men removed two hundred pictures. They also broke
some of the stained glass windows and defaced part of the font.
It was in 1672 that the ecclesiastical authorities gave permission
for our small church to be built from the stone of the old building since the earlier one had proved too large and costly to
maintain.

Wrentham is chronicled to a greater extent than Covehithe,
being, no doubt, a larger place. There was a village there in
Saxon times, in fact there were probably two close together, divided by a stream. Some historians think that Wrentham means
'divided village', but it was split into six manors.

By 1085, Wrentham was six manors whose area covered just
over two thousand acres, all owned by William de Varennes,
one of William the Conqueror's knights. He later became earl of
Surrey. He was followed, in the fourteenth century, by the earls
of Pembroke. By Elizabeth I's reign the manor was in the hands

163

of the Brewster family who built Wrentham Hall. It is no longer there but used to stand near Blackmoor Farm. The last of the Brewsters to live in the hall died in 1797 and, when Sir Thomas Gooch, the 4th Baronet, bought the estate in 1810, the hall was demolished. A few years earlier, in 1786, a new road was built through Benacre, across the newly drained Kessingland marshes to the fishing villages of Yarmouth and Lowestoft. In those days the Spread Eagle was a coaching inn on the new road.

The splendid hall built at Benacre by Sir Thomas Gooch, the 4th Baronet, was destroyed by fire in the 1920s but the rebuilt hall, in a similar architectural style, was the setting for the Benacre show.

Haymakers ready for work — early 1900s

Throughout the centuries, life in the English countryside and its villages has followed an annual pattern, largely determined by the seasons but also influenced by the vagaries of the weather. Other countries have a climate, they say, while we in Britain have weather. In every season there are tasks to be done; fields must be ploughed, seed has to be sown, crops are grown and harvested and then the cycle starts over again. To some extent the weather can affect when these jobs are done, but there are certain fixed points to which we always worked, like Christmas and Easter. As youngsters we looked forward to some of these treats with which our year was punctuated; there was the Buff's tea, harvest festival, Christmas and the agricultural show at Benacre Park.

When preparations were being made for the show, I went along with my father. We took two horses and went to the area of the show ring, the animals having first had leather boots fitted to prevent them from damaging the turf. To the horses we harnessed a large grass-cutter and cut out the show ring, right in front of Benacre Hall. The horses were used for other pulling duties while around them various preparations went on. Stalls were put up and large marquees erected while the show people came in with the fair. They brought steam horses, chair-o-planes and, best of all, the beautiful and raucous steam organs.

On show day itself, a Saturday always in June, people began to file into the park at about nine in the morning, the dew still on the grass. Preparations for the event had been going on all week but the planning had been in hand since the day after the previous year's show. The weather was always excellent — or has time just mellowed my memory? The marquees for features like the flower and vegetable show and the fur and feather section were all ready along with the paraphernalia necessary for such a show. It was very much an agricultural affair with classes for various types of cattle, sheep and horses. Pigs and goats also featured as did Pony Club events and show-jumping, but the people of Covehithe were far more interested in things like 'Best Cockerel in Show', 'Best Rabbit' and even 'Best Mouse'. The Foyster family always entered the flower show and, sometimes, the vegetable competitions. Wild flowers were our speciality. All of the Foyster children gathered them for several days before the show, our collecting ground being the marshes for that was where the rarest flowers grew. We always took care to set off the arrangement with a bloom known as a flaming poker and my sisters and I carried off several prizes.

My father always entered a Suffolk Punch mare and foal from the farm where he worked. I was allowed to lead the foal by its special white-rope show-head halter, and the first I ever led was a devil to hold. He led me rather than the other way round, but father, for all he was so much smaller that his charge, controlled her beautifully. I had to dig my heels into the ground to hold the foal still.

166

The agricultural show — early 1900s

Sulky-racing was very popular at the time, these being two-wheeled carts pulled by one horse. They seemed very precarious vehicles as they sped around the track, but their drivers managed to control them for most of the time.

Despite the fact that we were so far away from the great centres of population, the show had one great crowd-puller which some of the larger country shows would have been delighted to have. This was a magnificent display by the Household Cavalry who were procured for the day because of Sir Robert Gooch's strong connections with the regiment. They looked superb with their brilliantly polished helmets and breast-plates, their plumes and brightly coloured uniforms, and boots which shone in the sunlight. Their beautiful horses were greatly admired. These soldiers exchanged their uniforms later in the day to recall the days of the Wild West. They dressed up as cowboys and Red Indians and even had a stage-coach. The

167

Indians in the display rode bareback and the whole event was tremendously exciting with lots of shooting.

Their other party-piece was a demonstration of the use of the lance. They cleared jumps at the charge and showed off their tent-pegging skills.

I looked forward to lunchtime on show day because it was then that mother revealed the contents of the picnic basket. It had been carefully and secretly packed much earlier that morning. It must have taken some careful housekeeping and not a little ingenuity to have packed such a spread, for there was ham, chicken, cold sausages, several sorts of sandwiches, brown bread, cheese and pickle, apple pies, mince pies and fresh fruit, to recall just a few of that magic basket's delights.

I always made a particular point of staying close to the family on show day, but one day I did wander off to see what was happening in the fur and feather tent. My curiosity satisfied, I returned to where I thought the family was only to find to my horror that they were missing. All I could see, for I was very small, were legs and backsides, none of which I recognised. I was in a dreadful panic for what seemed like forever but was only a minute or so. Then I saw my mother's blue dress and charged towards it. We were reunited, but with so many people around, I refused to admit that I had been crying.

Harvest, which was a few months after the Benacre show, was another great time for the children, but it could be financially difficult for the adults. A harvest would be negotiated in those days and Suffolk farmers were notorious throughout England for being tight with their money. Many had a grand lifestyle themselves but wanted a great return on money invested in labour. The farmer and his men would meet to haggle and they usually agreed on a £5 harvest, in other words, a fixed-rate bonus for all the extra work involved in harvesting. If the workers could gather the harvest in good time, they would do well financially for they would be earning good money for the relatively few hours involved. Prolonged wet weather meant a very depressing time for the farm workers but, whatever the weather, the £5 bonus was paid in the end. To earn it they had

'Fourses' — afternoon break at harvest time

to start work at six in the morning and finish just before dark.
People, like my father, who were in charge of the horses worked
even longer hours. The horses had to be got in at 3.45 in the
morning and 'baited up', fed ready for work at 6. After their
day's work in the harvest field, the horses had to be returned to
the stables and fed for a good two hours before being turned out
into the horse-yard. These were all extra hours for the horseman to work and it was usually 11 o'clock at night before he
arrived home. The next day the whole procedure began again at
3.45 in the morning, so the horseman found little time for sleep.
The harvest work was very hard but the money earned was essential because with it the farm labourer could clothe and shoe
his children for the year ahead.

People in the late 1930s thought themselves well off in
comparison to their predecessors at the end of the nineteenth
century who would tell horrific tales of conditions before the invention of the binder. In Victorian days, a man was allocated a
specific amount of corn which he was expected to mow with a

The end of the day's work

scythe in a day; a good man could cut an area 60 rods long and 12yd wide in one day. The old people used to relate how a farmer would state how much he was prepared to pay for such exertion. It was very much a case of 'take it or leave it', but to have left it would have meant starvation. If one man would not do it for that amount, there was always another who would. The old people used to tell of a reverend gentleman who contended that to die by starvation was a divine thing, but, when challenged, he could name none of his persuasion who had so perished.

Using the scythe was a very difficult job and an art but before the invention of machinery it was the only way to cut the crops. Fields were much smaller then and the crop yields far less with poppies and weeds mixed in with the planted crop. The older men were experts with the scythe and there were frequently fourteen men in a field, along with a 'backer's boy', a school-leaver who would have a smaller scythe. He would take only a half of the tool's normal sweep. Behind all of these came women who tied the sheaves which were then stood up in stooks, several sheaves together.

By the time I first remember the harvest field, the binder had arrived but the headland of the field was still cut by the scythe for there had to be a space where the horses pulling the binder could walk. The binder cut the crop, bound it and dropped the sheaves behind it. Farm-workers then stood up the sheaves into stooks. These stooks were left until perfectly dry, when the waggons were brought into the harvest field. They were drawn by two horses, one in the shafts, the other in traces, but if the going was very heavy there could be two horses in trace, making three altogether. On the waggon was a man known as the loader who distributed the sheaves evenly as they were passed up to him. As lads, we loved to ride on the top of the load as it was taken to the stack-yard. Here it was shaped into a stack, an art in itself as the stack might have to stand there for some time. Different counties had their own individual ways of building stacks. When the stacks were up, they were thatched by the farm labourers. A properly thatched stack would withstand any winter without disintegrating. Some of the stacks would be taken down to be threshed just before Christmas as extra money was always needed by farmers then.

When the threshing tackle arrived, the thatch was removed. Two men with short forks climbed onto the stack while on the drum, part of the tackle, were another two. From the stack the sheaves were thrown down onto the drum whence they were passed on to the man known as the feeder. The bond holding the sheaf was cut by one of the drum men before it reached the feeder, a man who travelled with the threshing tackle and who fed the corn into the drum. If he ever made a mistake and fed it too much, the drum made a complaining sound and the man on the traction would glare a warning at him indicating that he did not expect such a happening again or heads would roll. The feeder also had to take great care that he did not slip into the drum himself for the beating blades would have made short work of him.

We loved to be around at threshing time for there were always hundreds of rats. They had been living in the stack and, as they desperately searched for a new hiding place, we set about them

171

with sticks. This reduced the rodent population and kept us busy for hours. Later in the year, during the winter, rat-catching became a lucrative pastime as we were paid a halfpenny for each rat's tail we delivered to the farmer. We used to take a ratting dog and a torch into the stack-yard and frequently caught dozens of rats. We kept only the tails which were delivered to the farmer. He gave us our money and took the tails to prevent our bringing them back a second time.

I was much happier chasing rats than I would have been working on the thresher because that was a filthy job. Various end products came out of different parts of the machine. The farm horseman would be on the end that received the corn. He would have a tumbrel ready and as each sack filled up with its 14 stones of grain it would be loaded into this cart which was then driven off into the granary. The men would lift these 14-stone sacks onto their backs and then run up a plank. When they reached the top they would shoot out the contents of the bag to join the rest of the corn already stored there. Robert Wright, the farmer's son, could carry two sacks on his back. He was enormously strong and adept at wielding these bulky weights, yet for all that he was not a particularly big man.

The grain which came out of the thresher chutes was graded as first, second, or third quality.

Another compartment on the drum was the chaff-cutter which did exactly what its name implied. This chaff was chopped up stalks which went into horse-bait.

At the back end of the drum was an opening known, in East Anglia at least, as the caulder hole and this had to be kept clear at all times. It was the dirtiest job of all and was almost invariably given to a boy. With his fork he had to continually clear away the unwanted weeds and seeds which had been harvested along with the corn.

The straw which was left at the end of the drum's activities was evicted from yet another hole and a few of the farm workers used to shape it into a stack; the whole process, then, converted the corn stack, via the drum, into a straw stack, grain and weeds having been extracted en route.

During their breaks from work, the older men would tell stories about harvest time in the old days. When 'all was safely gathered in' they looked forward to a harvest frolic, somewhat similar to that enjoyed by Thomas Hardy's characters in *Far from the Madding Crowd*. This tradition had died out by the 1930s but my father could remember it.

The barn would be thoroughly cleaned out and long trestle tables set up down the middle. There was food and drink provided and, afterwards, dancing to the music provided by a fiddler. Some farmers were very generous and provided half a bullock to be roasted over a spit. These frugal Suffolk farmers could be most lavish with their thanks when they felt a job had been done well.

When I see the combine harvester at work today, its driver sitting in a sound-proofed, air-conditioned cab listening to stereophonic music, I wonder what those old chaps with their scythes would have thought if they could see how their job is done now. Another difference is that whereas a modern combine harvester might have several different drivers in the course of harvest time, the scythe men would never let anyone use their scythe. It was a sacred tool and usually so well looked after that it could be used for the full length of the field without a sharpening. On his belt each man would have a little leather holder in which he kept his 'rub', a piece of light-coloured sandstone with which he sharpened his blade. This rub was very delicate and was easily broken so it was taken from its holder only when necessary, used and put away again. Keeping the scythes sharp was a work of art.

The old scythers had a stone jar of home-brewed beer which they would place at the far end of the field. As they began to scythe, they fixed their eyes on the beer jar and then worked steadily towards it. On even a relatively warm day, by the time each man reached his beer jar he was perspiring furiously and replaced the lost sweat with new-found beer. It was two more lengths of the field before he would again reach his refreshment. Each jar would hold a gallon so it would last a man a considerable time and he would not become drunk because he was sweating out as much as he was drinking. The scythe men always worked with their waistcoats on and would not remove them for fear of getting cold in their back. They also tied string around their trouser legs just below the knee to keep them well above their boots. Red flannel was worn next to the skin, particularly on the back, again to avoid getting cold, a ploy employed by other workers in other parts of Britain.

Harvest festival at Covehithe church was always on the morning of the first Sunday after the harvest was completed. Corn was always used to adorn the church as were vegetables and wild flowers, the overall effect being very beautiful and the service was always well attended. The fruit and flowers were afterwards sent to the cottage hospital at Southwold.

People nowadays look back nostalgically to what they re-

Loading the cart at hay-making

member as the romance of pre-war harvest times but there was a dark side, too. The work was hard and for little gain, but the money earned was so essential that people could not survive without it and, once earned, it was never wasted.

There were hard times in those days but there were good times, too. Looking back now I feel that we, as children, were largely shielded from the bad and given a large share of the good. That situation changed very little as I grew from child-hood into manhood. Harsh realities did come my way but they seemed to appear gradually and all through my early life I had mentors to help me face them. My father and mother nursed my first years, then came old Prod and, in his own way, my head-master, followed by Friday and Herbert Thrower. To all of them I owe a large debt and one I never realised I did owe until many years later. I was never asked to repay the debt but I have come to realise its very high value.

11

An End and
a Beginning

Herbert Thrower, the head keeper, was a man who showed me great kindness despite having had personal sadness of his own to contend with. To reach his house I used to pedal along Benacre Lane from my home in Covehithe. I cycled past Holly Common and through a wood to arrive at his rather superior keeper's lodge which was built of red brick and stood in the centre of a clearing in the wood. In his large yard stood the most enormous chestnut tree I had ever seen; its canopy shaded all the yard and the surrounding sheds and I imagined that it must have been beneath such a tree that the village smithy I had heard of in school poetry lessons must have stood as he plied his trade. Mr Herbert's house was larger and more imposing than the other keepers' dwellings. He was, after all, the head keeper. When Sir Robert used to shoot that beat the guns always had lunch in one of Mr Herbert's big rooms. He was not expected to provide the lunch, just the facility in which it could be comfortably consumed. On other beats, farmhouses were used for this meal because the rest of the keepers' cottages were too small.

During my time with Mr Herbert, I used the keeper's hut, again in the shade of the chestnut tree, as my base. I rarely went into his house but the hut itself was rather grand with wood panels and it was warm, too. I would leave all my gear in there, including my gun.

Mr Herbert was a widower whose house was kept for him by his daughter. She was a widow who had been married to the butler at Benacre Hall, Mr Ladbroke. Their son, young Pip, became part of the keepering staff and eventually took over Friday's beat and lived in his lodge. He, too, is now dead; apparently, he came home after a day's shooting feeling extremely tired, retired to bed early and died. He was younger than I and a very pleasant lad.

The beat nearest to Benacre Hall was known as the home beat and the keeper there was a grand chap called Doddington who suffered from an ulcer. He was treated in hospital and although he had to be careful about what he ate afterwards, he still liked a pint.

When the war eventually broke out, those keepers who were not required for active service became special constables. They already had a close link with the local police and were the obvious men for the job.

Doddington was always ready with a joke and there was never a shortage of pheasants on his beat. I wondered if they liked his sense of humour, too, but I knew that he was simply an excellent man with the pheasants and shooting day on his beat was always very good sport. This was despite the fact that the woods in his charge were on heavy land but he could both raise and hold his pheasants. I always enjoyed working with him even though he frequently pulled my leg.

Another keeper, whose territory bordered the home beat at the west end of the estate, was George Thrower, Mr Herbert's son. He was very energetic and a terrific walker. One of his greatest skills was in rearing partridges.

Bordering him, on the south Cove beat, was a man with the very distinctive name of Royal Martin. He was tall, skinny and rather stooping, and suffered from rheumatism. I disliked his father, Croombes Martin. Most of his family seemed to work at Benacre Hall in some capacity or other.

Billy Foulkard, known as Old Billy, had the smallest and poorest beat. It included the heathland area near Warren House and also encompassed one big wood. Being near the shore-line, these trees were bent from the strong north-east winds which blew in from the sea. It looked as if the old trees were permanently leaning away from these fierce winds. The large areas of heath and bracken presented a daunting and near hopeless task for the old keeper for if his birds dispersed and went into it their recovery would be almost impossible. For this reason he was never given as many birds as the other keepers but nevertheless, he managed to put on a good shooting day. Billy enjoyed telling stories about courting couples in the bracken and I often wondered how many he disturbed.

All of the keepers were excellent as workmates and pleasant as well; no one shouted at my inexperience and I could not have hoped for better companions and tutors. When I was wrong they quietly put me right and all of them always listened if there was something I wanted to say.

Life was good to me in every way and I was largely unprepared for the guillotine which was to end the old ways forever. Of course, we knew what Hitler was doing in Europe and we expected conflict ourselves, but how rarely do events take the course you expect.

The pheasant-rearing programme for 1939 was as usual. Friday was, by then, back at work and I had spent two years with Mr Herbert. The birds were raised and taken to the woods as in other years and in about the same numbers. Everywhere people were expecting the war to start. I was sawing wood for the cookhouse on the morning of Sunday, 3 September 1939. I was in the yard when Mr Herbert announced that we had declared war on Germany. This did not mean a great deal to me at that stage, but there followed the relative excitement of the blackout.

That season the shooting went off more or less as it had always done. One morning in November, Mr Herbert told me that there was no further work for me at Benacre. He found the situation harder to comprehend than did I. I must confess that, although I was not expecting the news, it somehow came as no great shock. It was as if I was being told that the war was on and I had better get on with it.

178

I was unemployed and needed no prompting to join up. Mr Herbert found employment for me at the Eagle Hotel in Wrentham. I went along to see the landlord, Mr Pack, and must have met with his approval for I was soon serving in the bar there and learning to be a waiter. At that time the area was flooded with troops, mostly the militia. They seemed to be everywhere and their officers, with their wives, took over the Eagle. I had the distinct impression that they were far more interested in their pink gins than in getting on with the war. Whenever the hotel was open, the bar was packed with troops and we pulled pints by the hundred. Almost every night we ran out of beer.

On one particular evening the bar was in its usual crowded state, full of shouting and banter. Several of the soldiers were waiting for drinks and one was resting his hand on the bar, drumming his fingers. Unfortunately, as it turned out, those fingers were too near the beer pump and as I was pulling a pint the mechanism squashed his fingers. He fainted and was carried out. What became of him I never found out. The other soldiers and staff reassured me that the accident had not been my fault, but I felt dreadful for weeks afterwards.

I was living at home then and found it quite difficult to move around the area. It seemed that wherever you went you were challenged by a soldier and we all had to put masks over our cycle lamps. Another disadvantage of all this military activity was that the local girls lost interest in us and began to pay great attention to the troops.

I was talking to the keepers one day and they advised me that if I was going to join the army I should try to get into a good regiment. From what I had seen of the militiamen, I could see what they meant, for they made anything but a good impression even on a youngster such as myself.

One evening, therefore, I sat down at the kitchen table and wrote a letter to the adjutant of the Life Guards, asking if I could join the regiment. As far as I was concerned, it was one of the best regiments and Sir Robert Gooch was the Colonel-in-Charge of the Household Brigade at that time. Although I did

'To-ho' — pointers at work, 1830s

not mention him in my letter, no doubt the connection was noticed from my Covehithe address. The adjutant replied within the week, writing that he would see what he could do for me. It was December and very soon I received an official reply instructing me to attend for a medical examination. Although still only seventeen, I had told them that I was eighteen. I passed the medical easily and was then sent my papers to report to Knightsbridge Barracks. My medical had been at Ipswich but here was the call to London. I was in the army, but it was not to last. The authorities discovered my real age and I had to return home for a couple of months.

I soon heard from them that they were forming a boys' battalion at Ipswich and this I eventually joined.

My boyhood was over. A boys' battalion it may have been but it was very much a man's life, and it was a long time before I again sat in the Suffolk countryside as a keeper, a good dog at my feet and a shotgun across my knees. In its place I was given a rifle and my old Wellingtons gave way to army boots. I had often grumbled about being soaking wet as I walked my Benacre beat, but there were occasions in the next few years when I would have stood out cheerfully in an all-day thunderstorm just to be back in Suffolk and hailed once more as the Boy Johnny.

Aftermath

Life on the Benacre estate did not come to an end just because I went away to war, but things did gradually change as the old order gave way to the new. Somehow I never thought of people like Friday and Herbert growing old, but they did, of course. Attitudes changed, too.

I returned after the war with something of a rebel attitude and although there would have been a job waiting for me at Benacre I did not feel inclined to take it. I did not want to join those unfortunate old people who felt that they had to lower their eyes when spoken to by their 'betters'. Even as a boy, I used to wonder why employees did not look their employer straight in the eye. Having been in the army and taught from the start to look my superiors straight in the eye when talking to them, I found the overt subservience at Benacre a little out of place. Mr Herbert was not guilty of it but he did carry considerable authority in any case. It was the lesser employees who were notably subservient and who seemed to lack confidence. Prod can have had little confidence in himself through his entire life. He had worked all his life for a pittance and when his working life was over he had nobody on whom to fall back for support. Most old people in the countryside relied on their families to look after them when they could no longer do so themselves and they were, in general, very well looked after. Those who had no

'Hi-seek' — pointers at work, 1830s

such support and who had been unable to save much money had but one destination and that was the local workhouse. This was where paupers ended their days and Prod was very definitely one of those. There was nothing for his kind to look forward to and all they had was their memories. I like to think that he managed to hang on to his old officer-of-the-watch telescope for that would surely have revived some memories. Exactly how and where he died, I do not know. It would have been best had he died in his hut, surrounded by his few worthless but familiar possessions.

Herbert retired during the war and went to live in a pleasant house in Mill Lane. It had a good garden in which he kept himself busy and I went to see him several times in my early days as a soldier. Rather sadly, when I went to see him in the 1950s, he did not recognise me. His grandson, Pip, took over one of the Benacre beats when he left the forces at the end of the war, but he, too is now dead.

Friday retired and died shortly after the war, as did old Billy.

Of my contemporaries from schooldays, very few are to be found in the Covehithe and Wrentham area today. Many of them perished in the war. Most had joined the Royal Norfolk Regiment and a large number of them failed to return after years of incarceration in a Japanese prisoner-of-war camp. Those who survived the experience came back in a pitiful state and few are alive today.

Retirement eventually came for Mr Spall, my old headmaster. I saw him briefly in 1946 and we had a long talk; he was pleased that I was branching out into the world, as he put it, for I was about to take up a job as a chancery guard servant. He did not believe in people leading a humdrum existence.

My best pal, Jack, had joined the Royal Army Medical Corps, was posted to Ireland and, after just a short time, contracted and died of meningitis in the very early part of the war.

I wrote once during the early part of the war to Georgina, the girl who walked the spaniels. She had joined the WAAF and at that time we all seemed to be guarding airfields. I was in Norfolk and she had been posted to the north of England. She replied to my letter telling me that she was trying to get a posting nearer to home, but then I was sent further afield and our brief exchange of letters ceased. She also told me that she had become engaged to be married.

Many of the girls of my generation and many of my female class-mates left Suffolk soon after the war to start a new life in America. They were GI brides who had married airmen serving on United States Air Force bases of which there were many in East Anglia during the war.

After the war, I decided that army life suited me. I liked the army and it seemed to like me, so we stayed together for more than twenty years. The funny thing was that, no matter where I was serving, I was never far away from gamekeeping. Those five years spent at Benacre Park training with Friday and Herbert helped me more than I can say during the war and in the years that followed. What they taught me was far more than a trade; it was an education for life.

There are times when I could swear that Friday and Herbert walk my beat with me still today, and the vision of old Prod, hotly pursued by those angry bees, still comes to mind now.

I still wonder, too, if it was indeed he who had sprung that other trap at Benacre Broad all those years ago. I never did find out for certain and I fear that now I never will. Let us simply say that it was one of life's sweet mysteries, a secret not to be fathomed by mortal men. It would never do if we knew all the answers to the questions life puts our way, now would it?

Acknowledgements

The authors would like to thank the following people for their invaluable assistance in the compilation of this book:

For the loan of photographs, Janet and William Pipe of Wren House Antiques, Wrentham, Suffolk; Robin Cook of Swainby, North Yorkshire; the landlord of the Five Bells, Wrentham; Liz and Tony Dodds of William Dodds, Tubwell Row, Darlington, Co Durham.

For constant encouragement, Elizabeth Steele, Curator, Raby Castle, Staindrop, Co Durham.

For typing and correction of the manuscript, Barbara Proud, and for refreshments provided in abundance during the writing of the book, Trudy Foyster.

For additional photography, Neville Turner of Barnard Castle.

Index